Trains
to the
West

Trains
to the
West

George Heiron

LONDON
IAN ALLAN LTD

First published 1978

ISBN 0 7110 0866 3

© Ian Allan Ltd 1978

Published by Ian Allan Ltd, Shepperton, Surrey,
and printed in the United Kingdom by
Ian Allan Printing Ltd

Introduction

Never before in the field of photography has so much money been spent or so much film been expended on railways as in the past few years. It is evident that with such a wide range of sophisticated photographic equipment and films available nowadays, more and more people are taking advantage of the situation and losing no time in recording on film the rapidly changing railway scene. It is to be hoped that there will always be a railway system to serve this country, but the continuing pruning of route mileage, withdrawing of trains and closing of stations is bound to give cause for concern.

In this album of photographs taken on the Western Region, I have set out to portray the atmosphere and spirit of the railways from the 1950s up to the present day with the Inter-City 125 HSTs. The present frequent day-long service of fast Inter-City expresses is certainly advantageous to the travelling public and a far cry from the 1950s, when only a selected few trains kept a fast schedule, but it is no consolation to the photographer who looks for something more ambitious than the hourly procession of regimented Inter-City 125s! What chance has he, the artistically inclined, of finding the varied and interesting railway scenes of the steam era in today's vastly streamlined and standardised affair, where all the once familiar lineside 'features' such as semaphore signals, and the inevitable lengthmen are conspicuous by their absence? Even the very track itself has, by and large, lost its attractiveness; the wooden sleepers and manicured ballast, once religiously maintained in immaculate trim by competing track gangs, has been superseded by ugly concrete sleepers covered by a copious amount of large-gauge ballast. The generally busy image of yesteryear has given way to comparatively austere conditions; therefore, the photographer must adjust his approach to picture-taking accordingly. For instance, where once the abundant lineside objects provided the accessories to the main subject, now more effective use must be made of the surrounding natural landscape to strengthen the picture.

Indeed, a diesel picture does need strengthening, as aesthetically the diesel locomotive presents a rather disappointing aspect when viewed from the normal track-level three-quarter angle. Its large flat sides and ends, which resemble a motor lorry cab rather than a railway locomotive, cannot compare with the steam engine bristling with detail and 'alive' with smoke and steam. Even a non-railway enthusiast could not resist the urge to whip out his camera at the sight and sound of a steam-hauled express!

Right from the time that I started railway photography with a Brownie box camera in 1945, I have always endeavoured to maintain a picturesque approach in sunlight, rather than the purely technical record. Night scenes, I think, are particularly effective, especially in wet conditions, when trackwork, platforms and coach roofs glisten under station lights. An otherwise ordinary station scene can be transformed into a sparkling magic world in a fine steady drizzle — on celluloid if not literally!

Station exteriors, with their adjacent bus terminals, do not escape my attention through the lens, and I find a certain fascination in station booking halls and restaurants during busy periods. On occasion I stand in a crowded swaying coach or restaurant car 'hiding' from questioning gaze behind the viewfinder of my camera, and sometimes evoking remarks about 'candid camera' from the seated occupants.

A complete contrast to these crowded areas are the lonely miles of open countryside through which the line passes. Imagine a remotely situated colour-light signal in the silent small hours of the morning. A full moon is rising from the mist, its yellow light reflected in the polished rail tops, while on the stillness of the night comes the distant hooting of owls. The signal flicks to green and after a few minutes a faint clatter rapidly grows into an earth-shaking crescendo of sound as a sleeper express passes by on its journey through the night. Experiences like this encourage me to remain active in this rewarding game of railway photography.

So climb aboard *Trains to the West* and commence your journey when the 'Britannias' were new, travel the rails down through the years on the 'Blue Pullman', ride behind a Class 52 'Western' diesel-hydraulic and arrive at your destination in an Inter-City 125.

Above: Bright periods with occasional showers might well have been the weather forecast for this spring day in 1953 as 'Castle' class 4-6-0 No 5037 *Monmouth Castle* hurries the 1.30pm Bristol-Paddington along near Hullavington, Wilts.

Right: No 1004 *County of Somerset* in the roundhouse at Swindon.

Above: Giant thunderheads drift in the blue and the surrounding hills resound to heavy stack music as the eastbound 'Merchant Venturer' blasts up the hill to Box Tunnel on 14 July 1954 behind a 'Castle' 4-6-0.

Above right: The driver of 'Castle' 4-6-0 No 7000 *Viscount Portal* gives his gleaming mount a spot of oil while waiting for signals at Swindon.

Right: The down 'Merchant Venturer' rattles through Chippenham behind No 7024 *Powis Castle* on 8 June 1953.

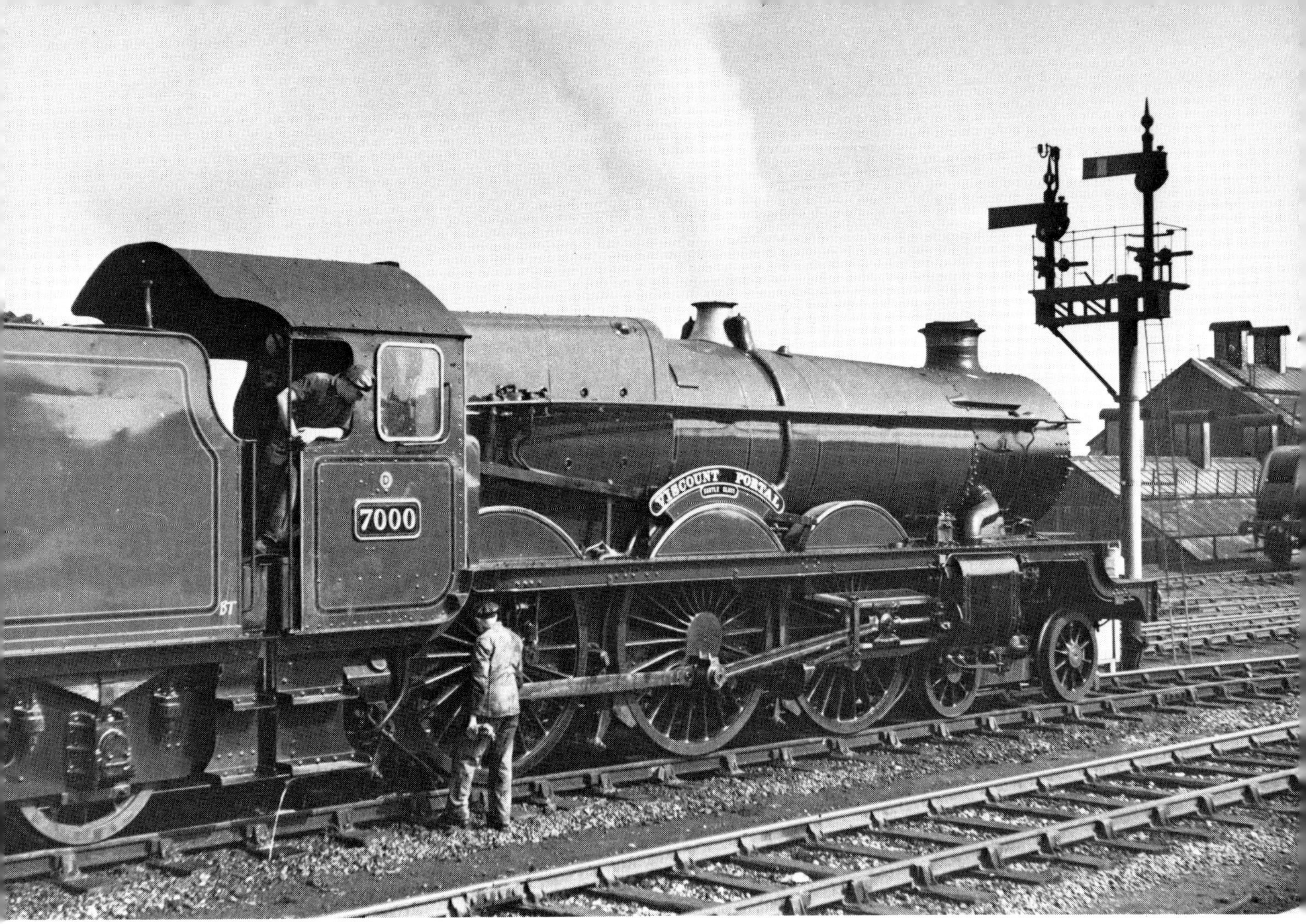
7000
VISCOUNT PORTAL

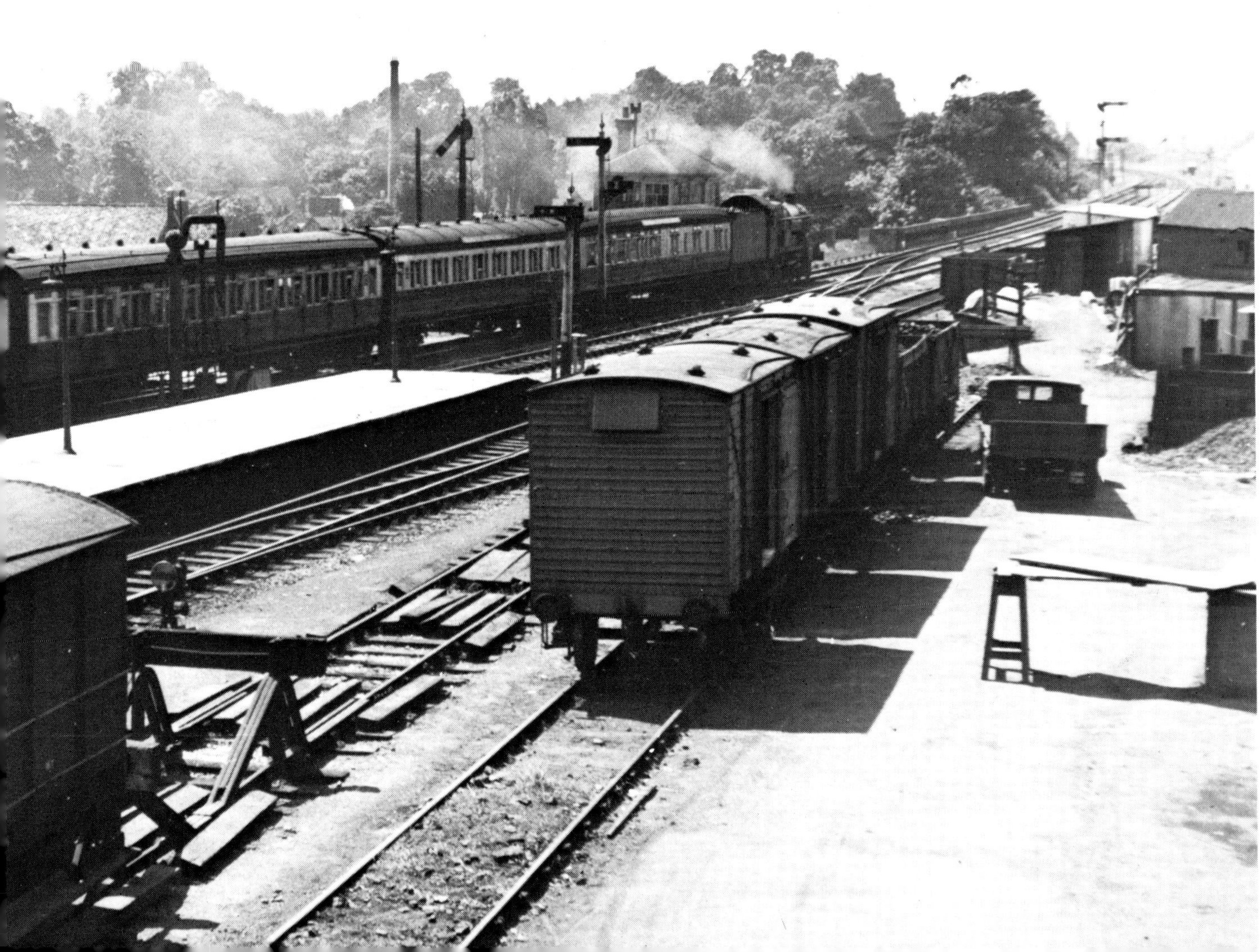

Above: 'County' class 4-6-0 No 1019 *County of Merioneth* gallops out of Fox's Wood Tunnel, east of St Anne's with the 2.38pm Bristol-Bradford-on-Avon stopping train in August 1957.

Left: No 7029 *Clun Castle* passing through Bath with the 'Farewell to Steam' special on 27 November 1965.

Right: No 5073 *Blenheim* emerging from Box Middle Hill Tunnel with the 1.15pm Bristol-Paddington express in June 1962.

Below: Class 7 Pacific No 70023 *Venus* streaks out of Box Tunnel with the westbound 'Bristolian' on Thursday 18 September 1952.

Below right: The village of Box makes an attractive backdrop to this unusual view of a 'County' class 4-6-0 leaving Box Middle Hill Tunnel with a Paddington-Bristol train.

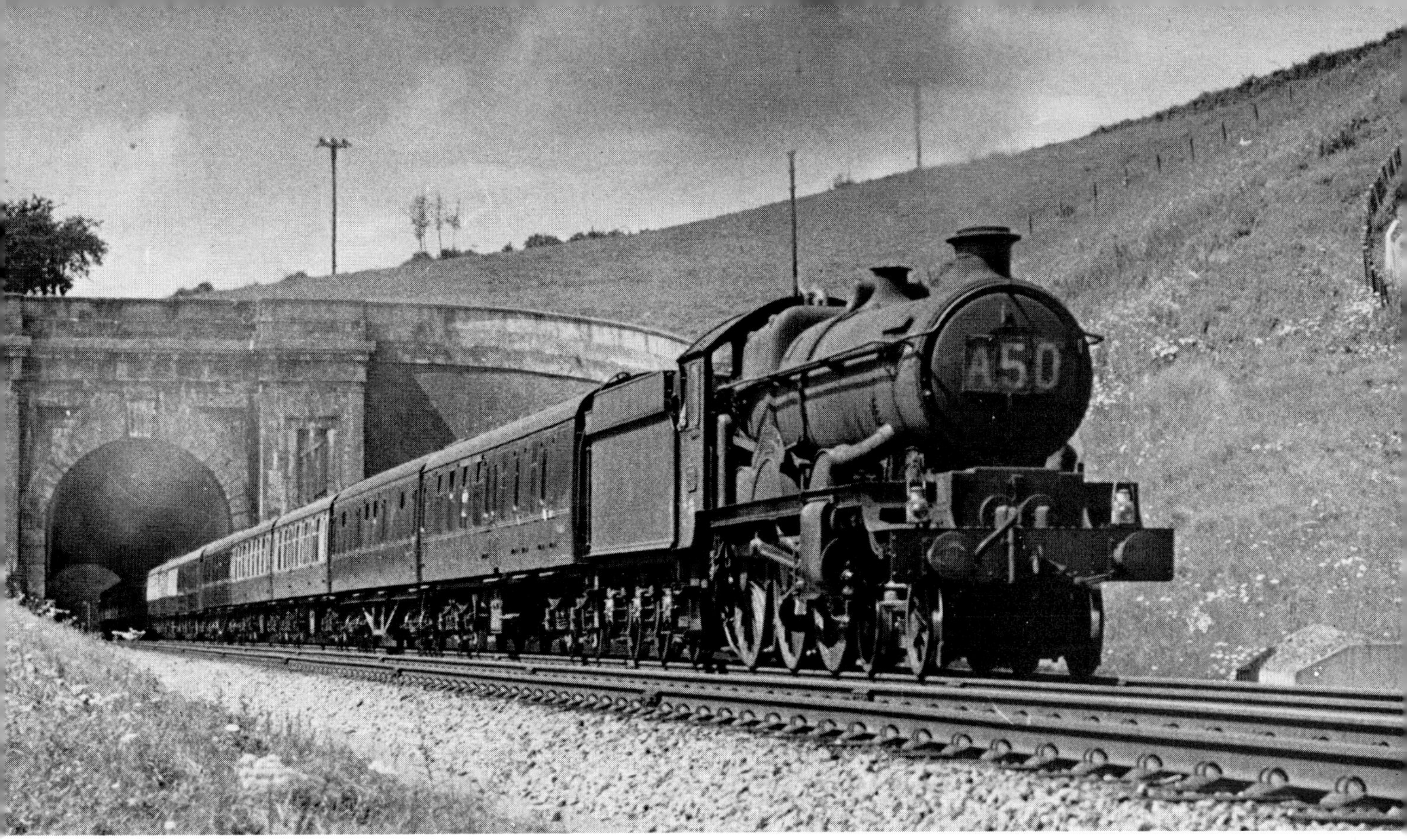
A50

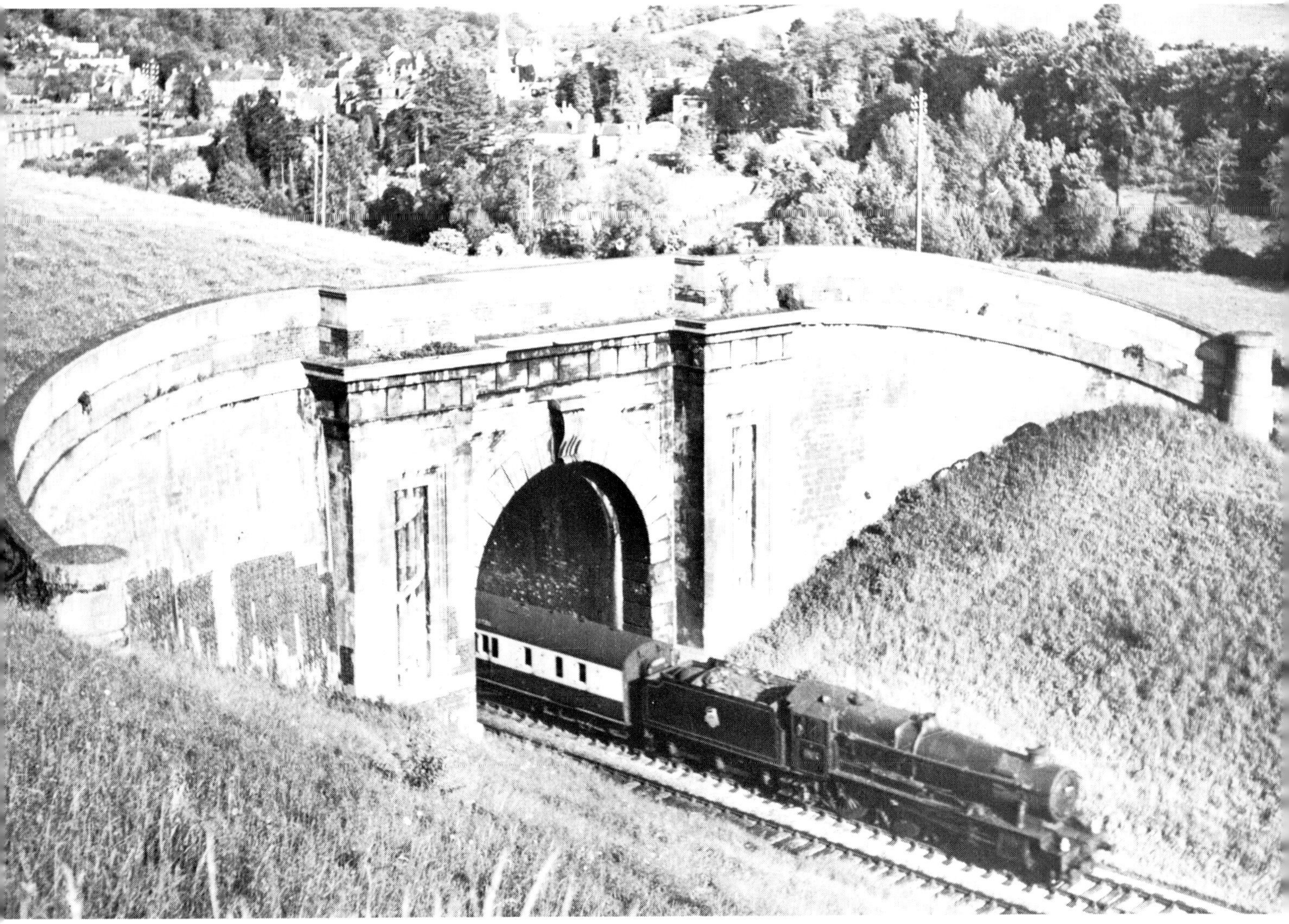

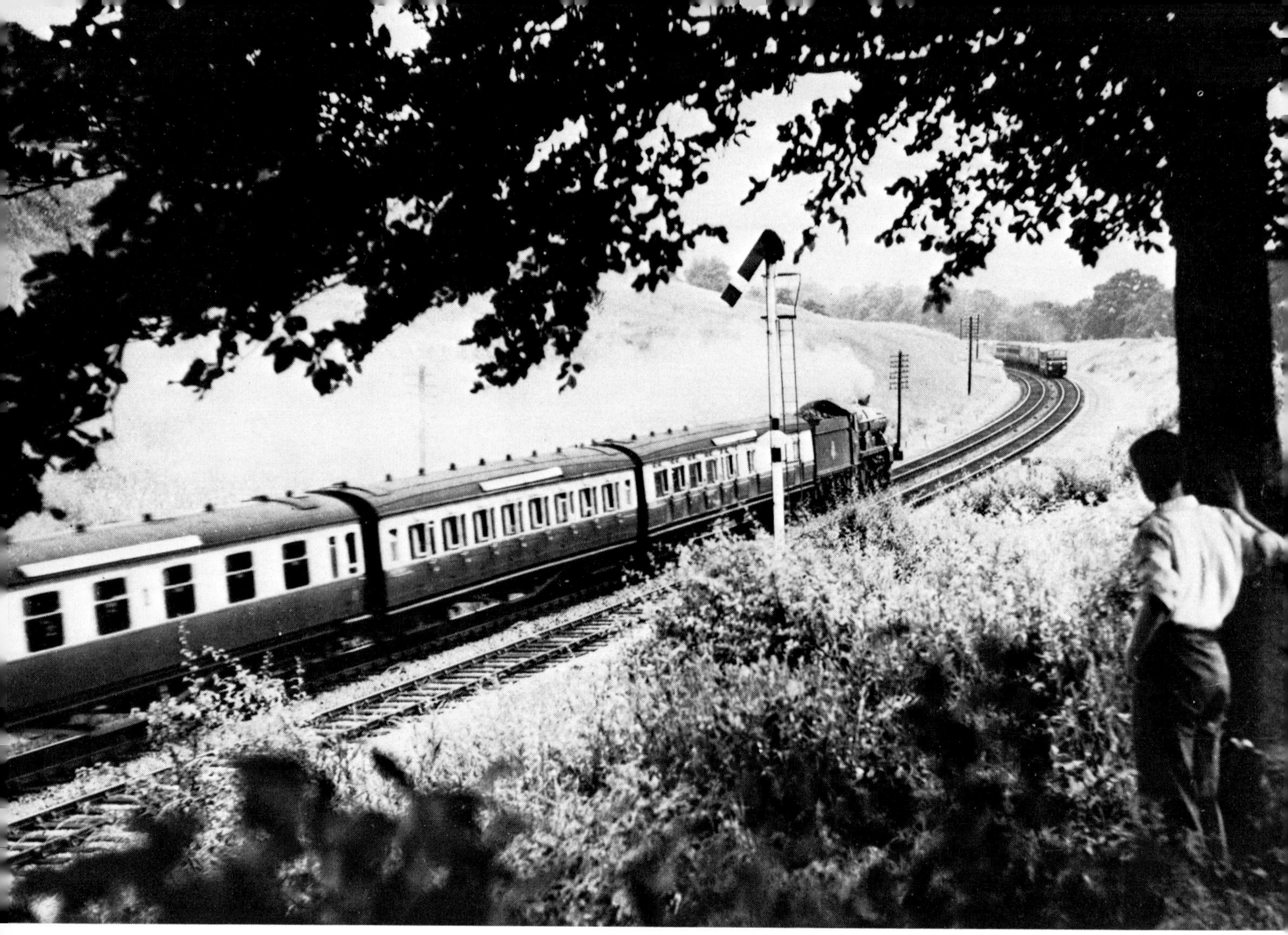

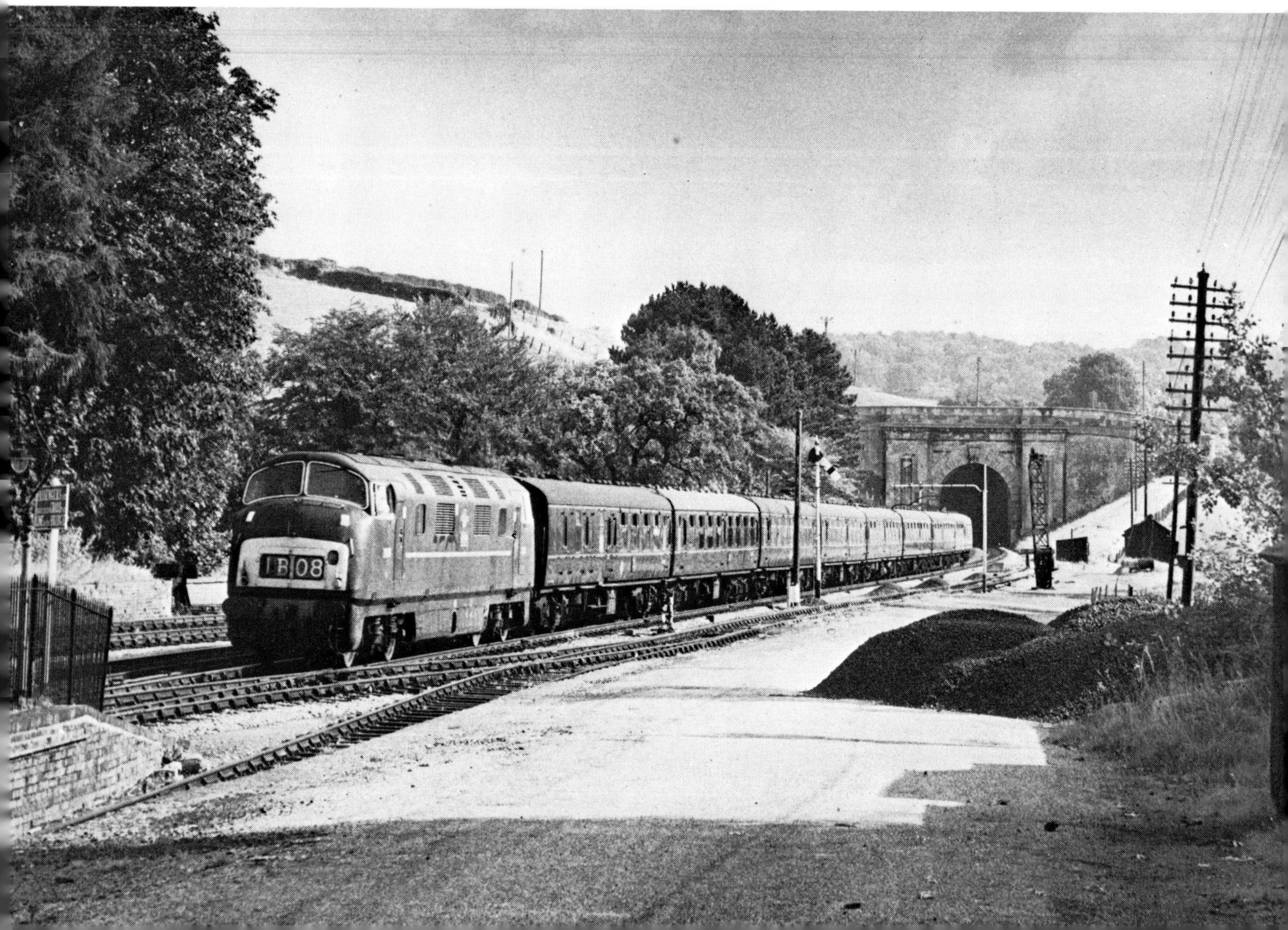
1B08

Above left: A 'Castle'-hauled Paddington-Plymouth express meets an eastbound express headed by Metrovick gas turbine No 18100 on Box Hill.

Left: A 'Warship' diesel-hydraulic races down from Box Middle Hill Tunnel at the maximum permitted 75mph with a Paddington-Bristol express in late September 1963.

Above: A 'Hymek' diesel-hydraulic heads a Paddington-Weston-super-Mare express through Box station in June 1962.

Left: The 3.15pm Bristol-Paddington express headed by a 'Western' diesel-hydraulic, about to pass under Shockerwick footbridge, on the way up to Box Tunnel in June 1966.

Above: A Weston-super-Mare-Paddington express passes Box behind a 'Warship' class diesel-hydraulic in June 1961.

Above: The weather-beaten ramparts of Twerton Tunnel stand guard over Brunel's imperial way as Metrovick gas turbine No 18100 enters the west portal with the up 'Bristolian'.

Above right: A BR standard Class 3 2-6-2T at Box station with a Swindon-Bristol stopping train.

Right: A 'Castle' class 4-6-0 roars up through Box with a heavy Bristol-Paddington express in June 1962.

Above: The westbound 'Merchant Venturer' hurries down from Box Tunnel behind a 'Warship' diesel-hydraulic in June 1961.

Above right: The ground trembles to fast-moving tonnage as 'King' class 4-6-0 No 6016 *King Edward V* rushes out of Box Tunnel at 80mph with a Paddington-Plymouth express.

Right: Looking like a pantomime backdrop, the west portal of Twerton Tunnel is bathed in evening sunlight as 'King' class 4-6-0 No 6017 *King Edward IV* emerges with a Swindon-Bristol stopping train.

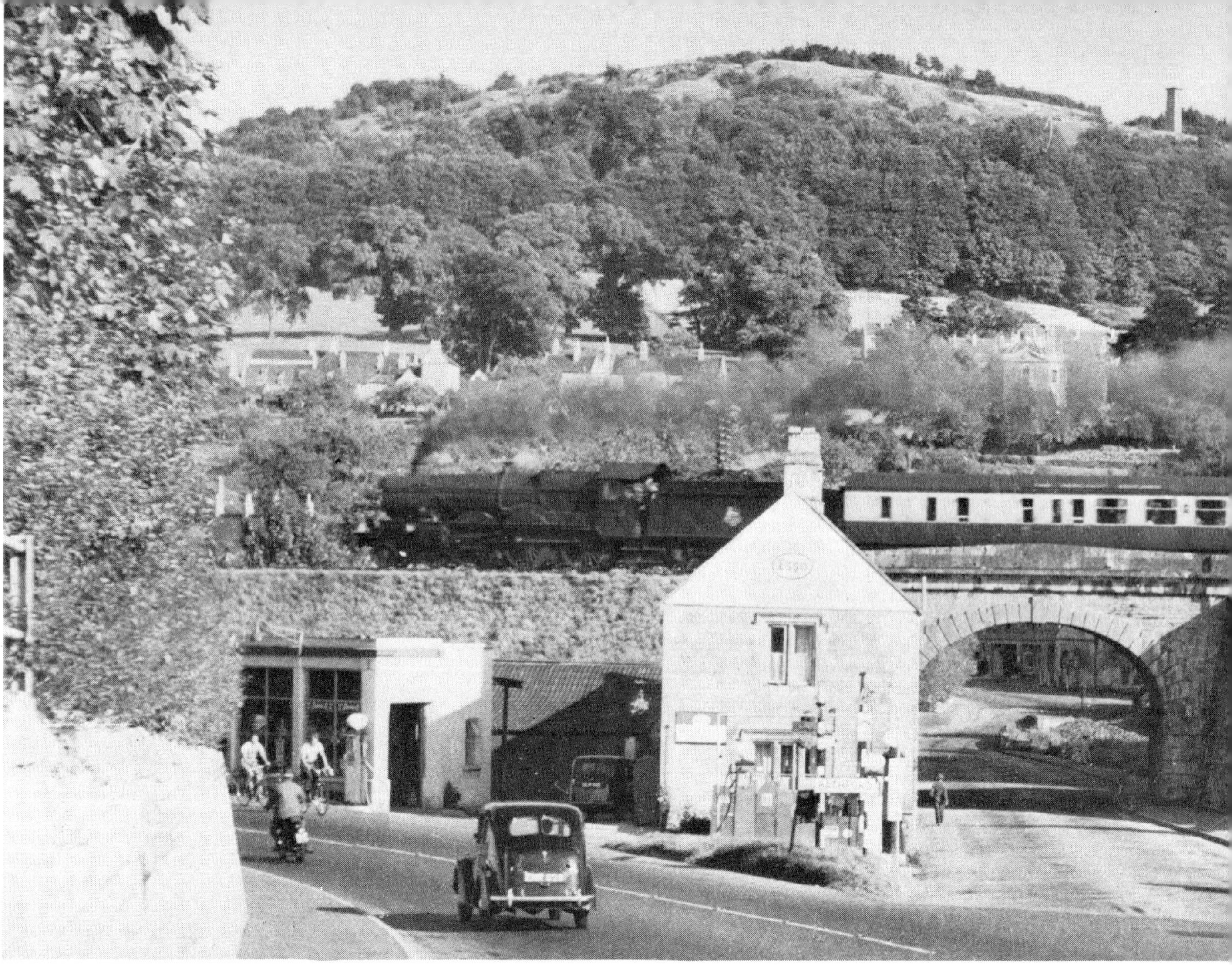

Left: The eastbound 'Merchant Venturer' speeds over the road to Bradford-on-Avon (the London road forks to the left) on the way up to Box Tunnel.

Below left: A Collett 2-6-2T with 5ft 8in driving wheels pushes hard on the tail of a freight climbing the 1 in 60 to Sapperton Tunnel.

Below: No 7035 *Ogmore Castle* and a sister 'Castle' 4-6-0 double-head a South Wales-Paddington train climbing Sapperton Bank, diverted from the normal Badminton route because of engineering work in the Severn Tunnel.

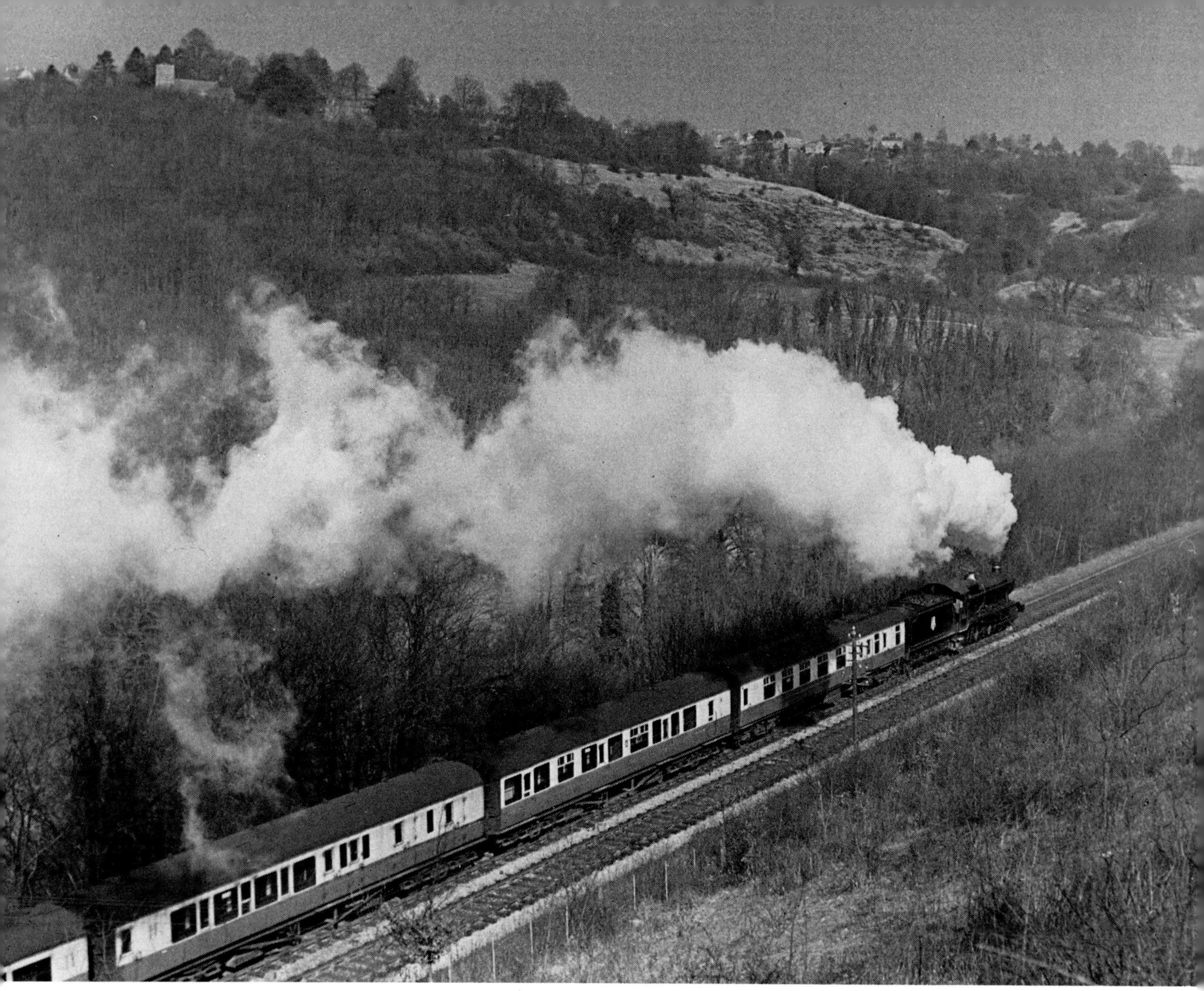

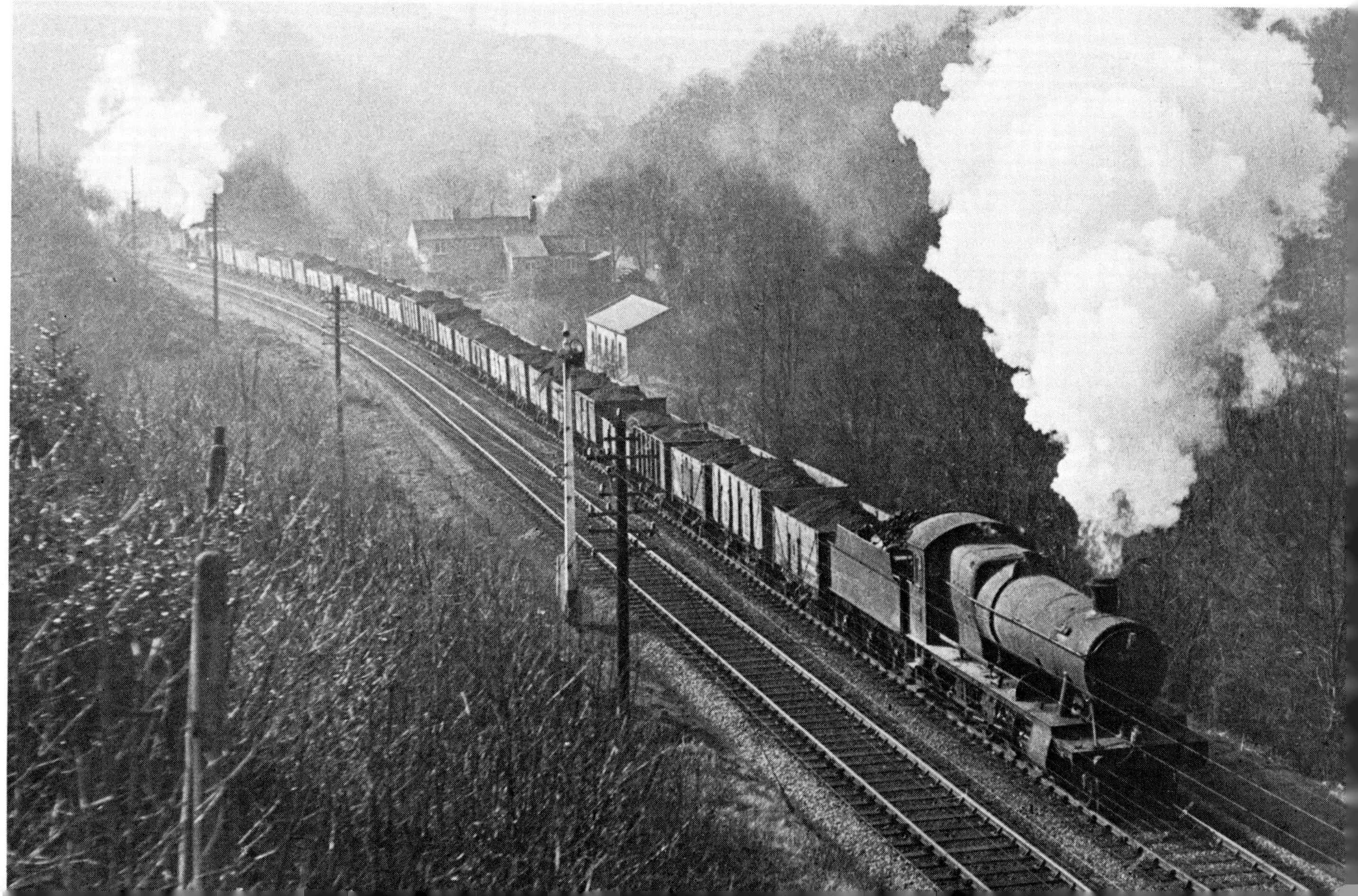

Above left: 'Hall' 4-6-0 No 5980 *Dingley Hall* blasts up the 1 in 60 of Sapperton Bank east of Chalford with the 2.10pm Cheltenham-Swindon stopping train in February 1956.

Left: A South Wales-Swindon coal train, headed by 2-8-0 No 3819, climbing Sapperton Bank in the early 1950s.

Above: On a misty day in December Class WD 2-8-0 No 90544 labours up Sapperton Bank, slipping spasmodically on the greasy rails, with a coal drag in tow.

Above: The quiet of a May morning is shattered by the thunderous exhausts of 'Castle' class 4-6-0 *The Gloucestershire Regiment 28th 61st* and 2-6-2T No 5182 as they take a bend at 60mph with the eastbound 'Cheltenham Spa Express' on the 1 in 60 gradient up to Sapperton Tunnel in May 1959.

Above right: WR 2-6-2T No 3164 boosts a freight up the hill to Sapperton Tunnel on 3 March 1953.

Right: WR 4-6-0 No 5951 *Clyffe Hall* storms up Sapperton Bank with the 2.10pm Cheltenham-Swindon stopping train in January 1954.

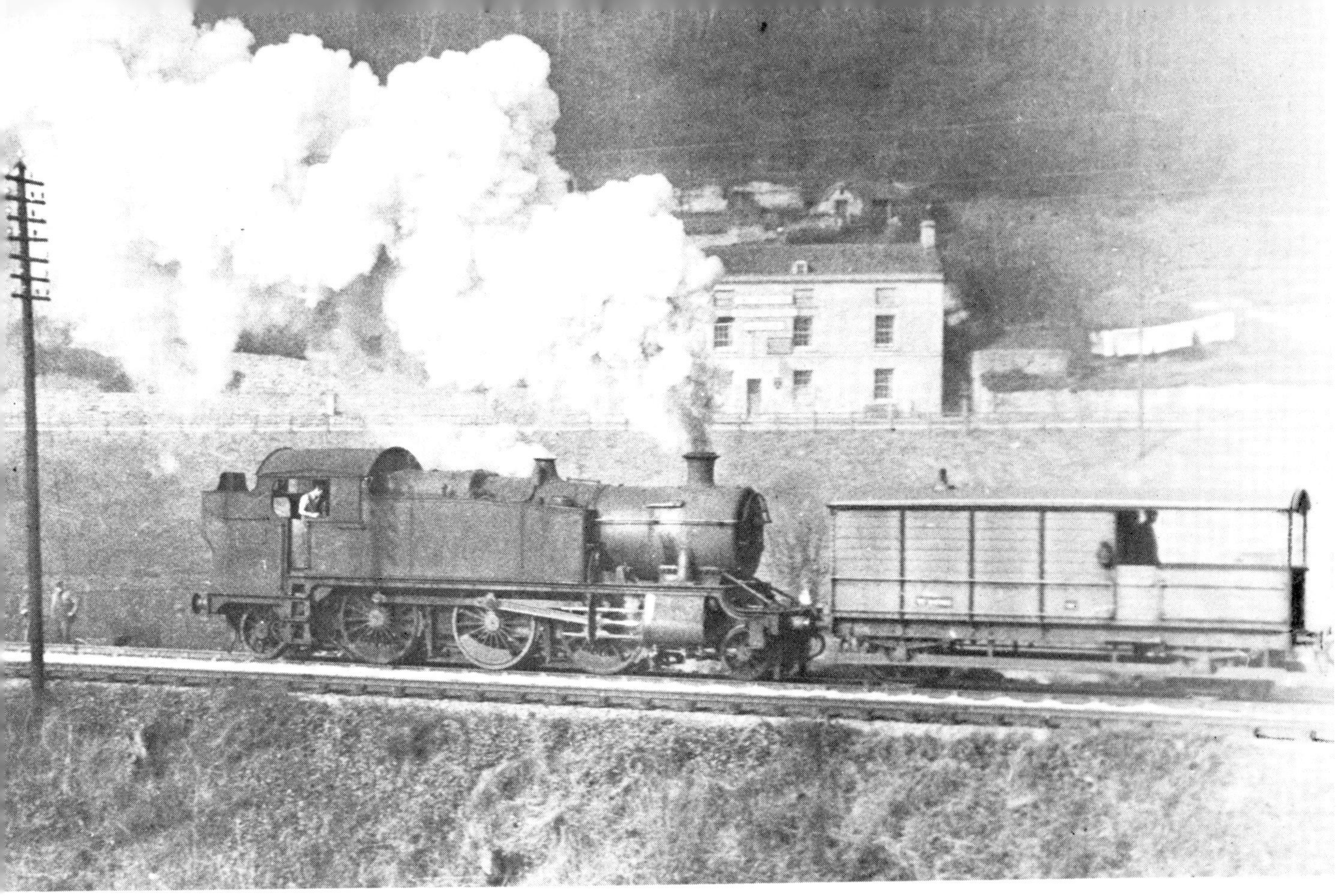

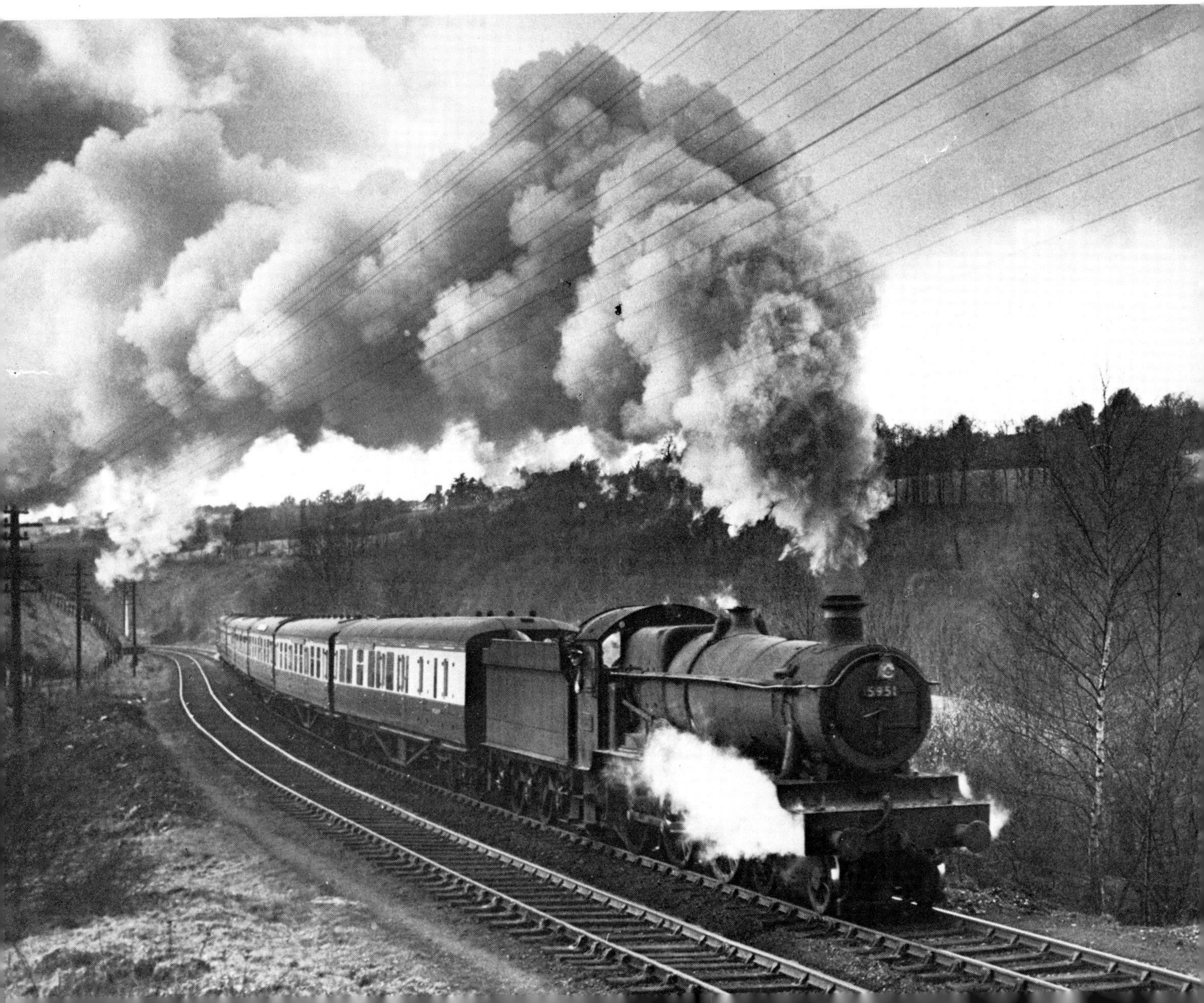
5951

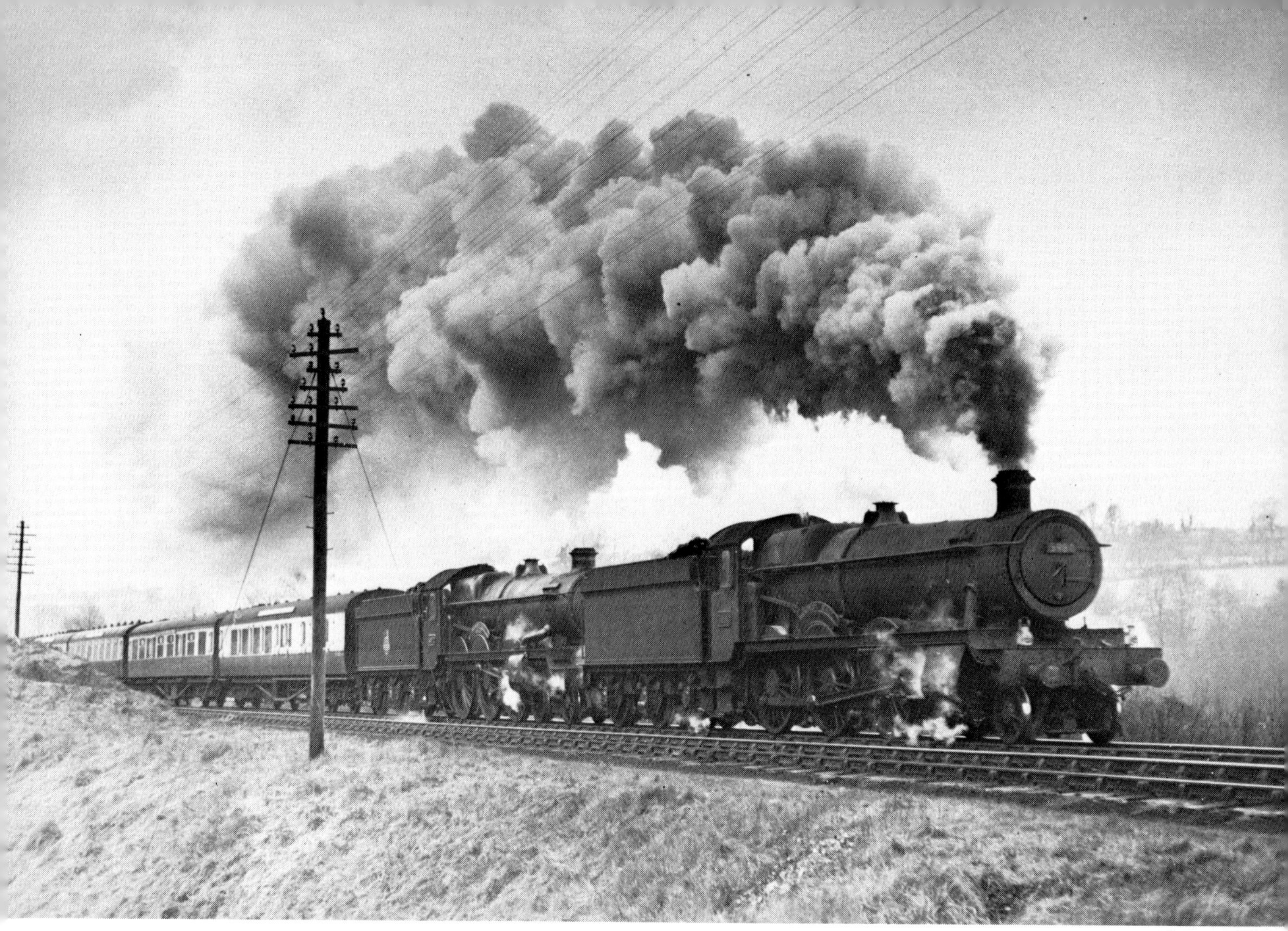

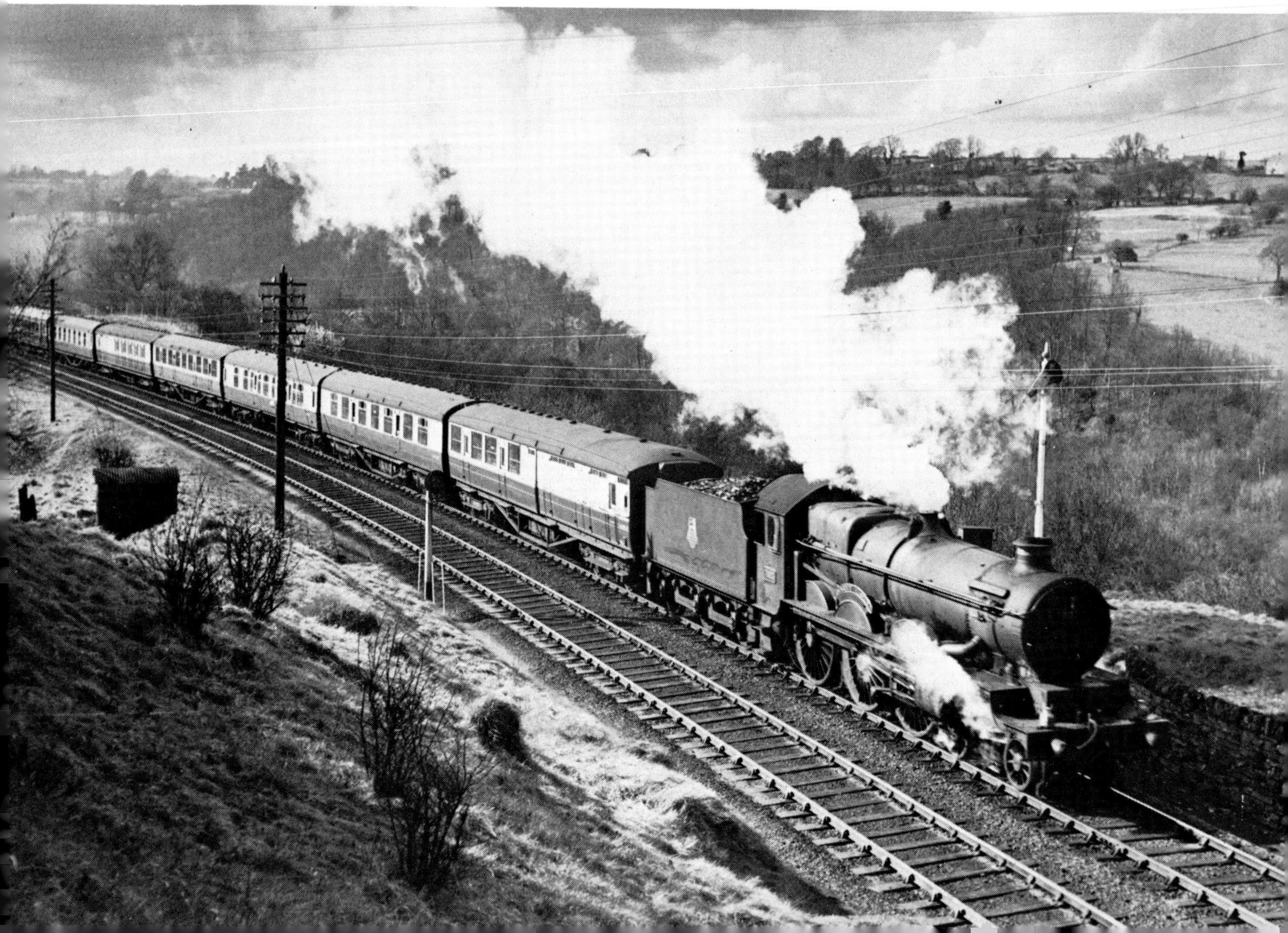

Above left: Nos 5980 *Dingley Hall* and 5072 *Hurricane* climb Sapperton Bank with a Sunday South Wales-Paddington express in February 1954.

Left: The battle of the big hill is about over for WR 4-6-0 No 7023 *Penrice Castle,* seen here about to enter Sapperton Tunnel with a London-bound express in April 1954.

Above: No 5007 *Rougemont Castle* on Sapperton Bank above Chalford with the Sunday 12.35pm Cheltenham Spa-Swindon train in November 1961.

Right: The graceful Bath Spa station in the 1950s.

Below: A Paddington-Bristol express pulls out of Bath Spa station behind a 'Western' diesel-hydraulic on the morning of 29 October 1966.

Far right: 'Western' class diesel-hydraulic No D1039 *Western King* entering Bath Spa station with one of the hourly Bristol-Paddington trains in July 1965.

Below right: A Portsmouth-Cardiff dmu crosses the River Avon at Bath on a summer afternoon in the 1960s.

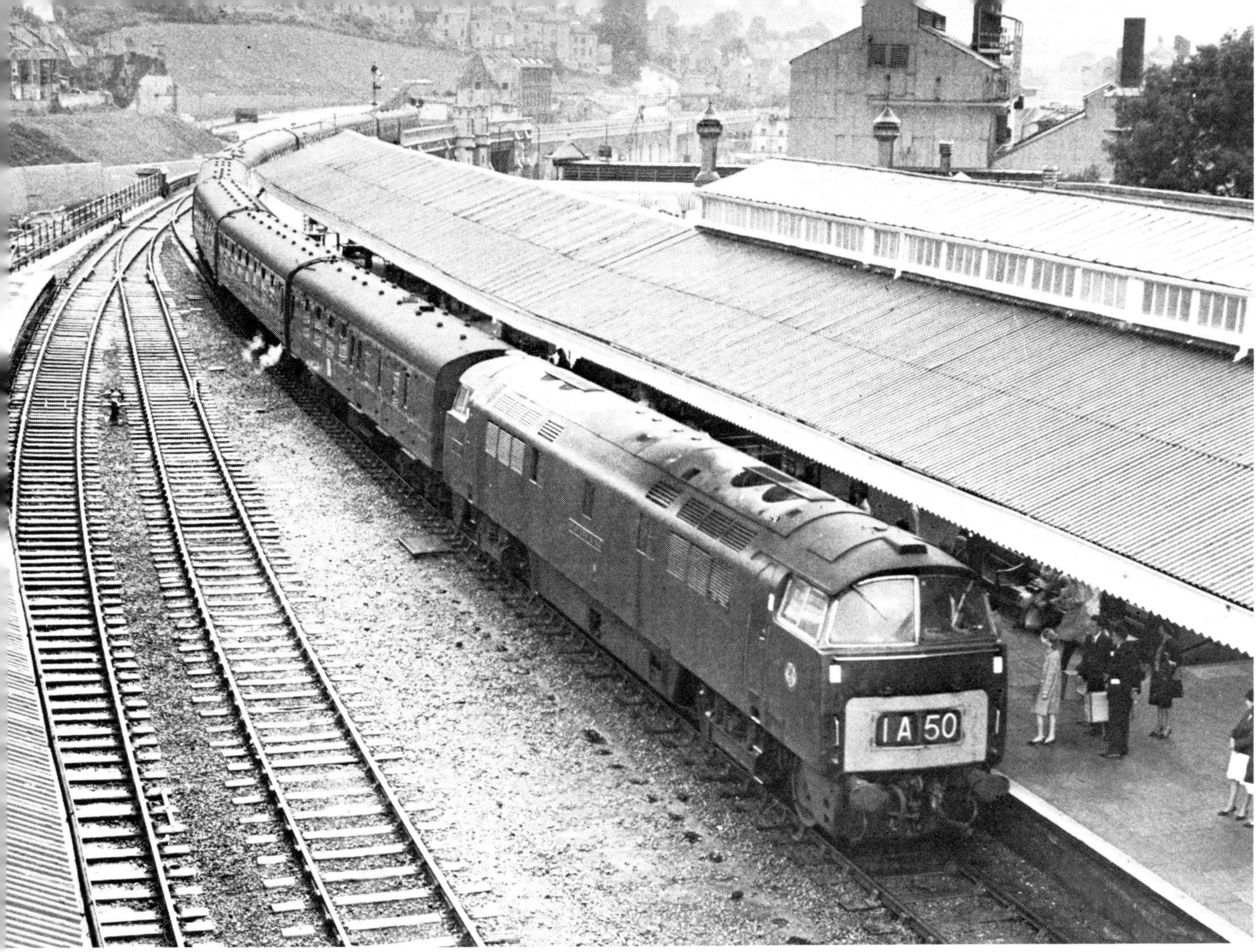
IA 50

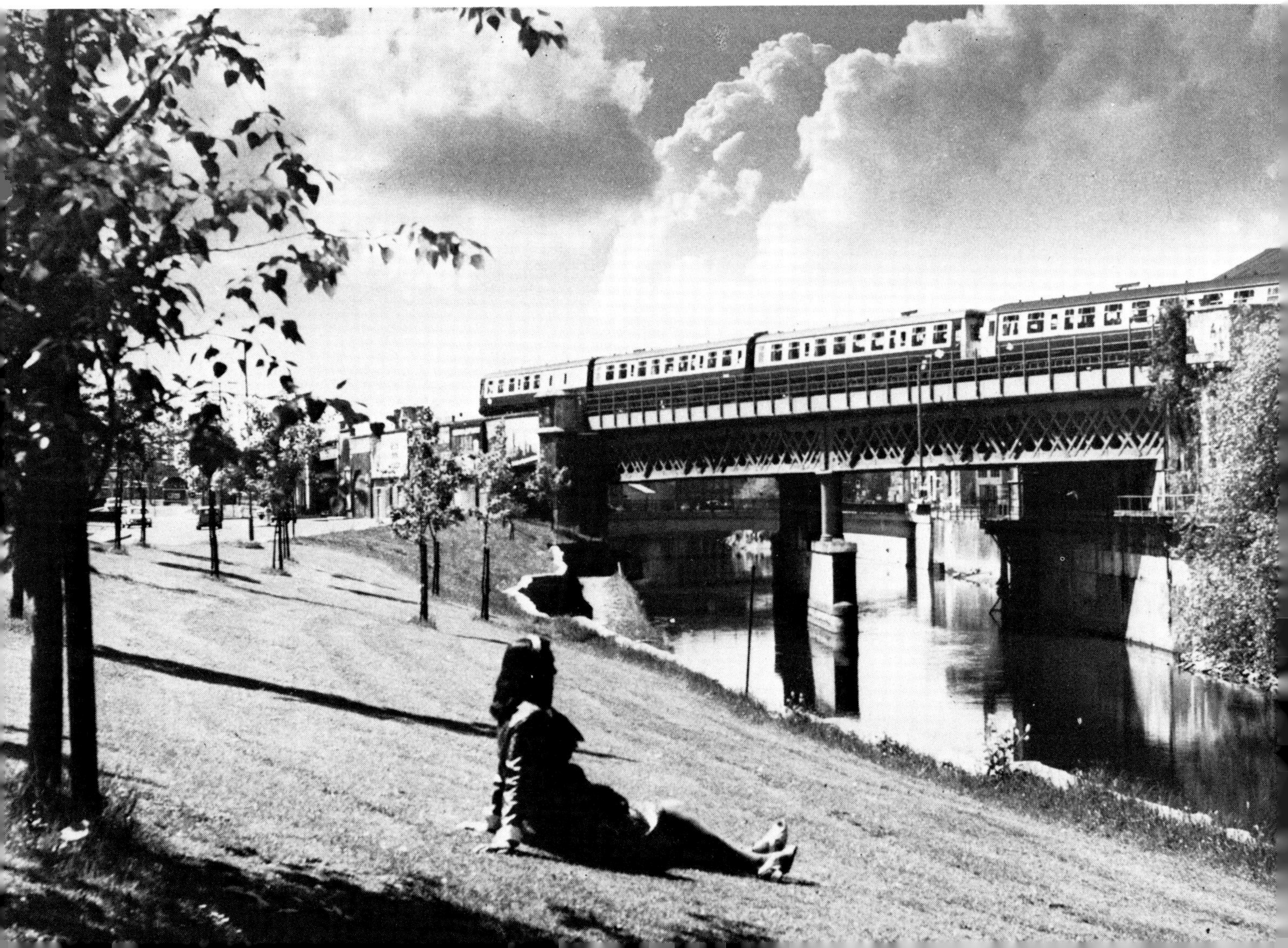

Above: A heavy fitted freight rumbles past Wapley sidings near Chipping Sodbury behind a 'Castle' 4-6-0.

Above right: Shades of night are falling fast as WR 4-6-0 No 6996 *Blackwell Hall* drags a westbound freight past the distant signal for Badminton station in August 1953.

Right: WR 2-6-0 No 9309 taken at speed in Chipping Sodbury cutting.

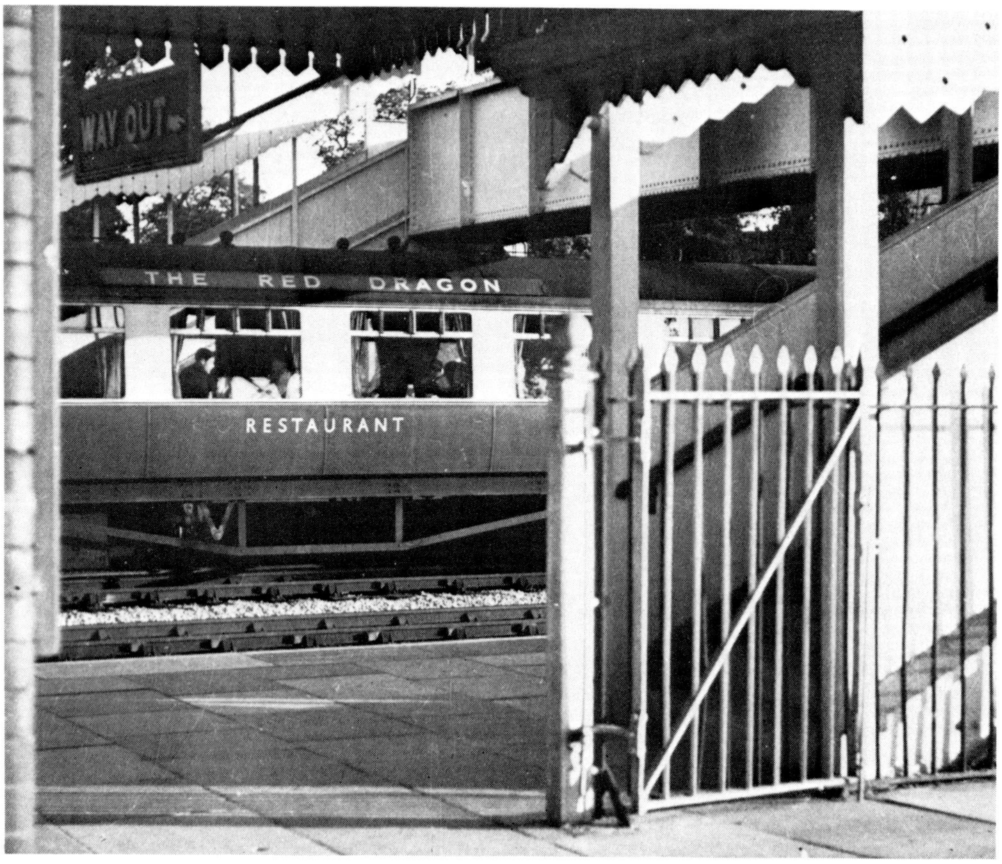
WAY OUT
THE RED DRAGON
RESTAURANT

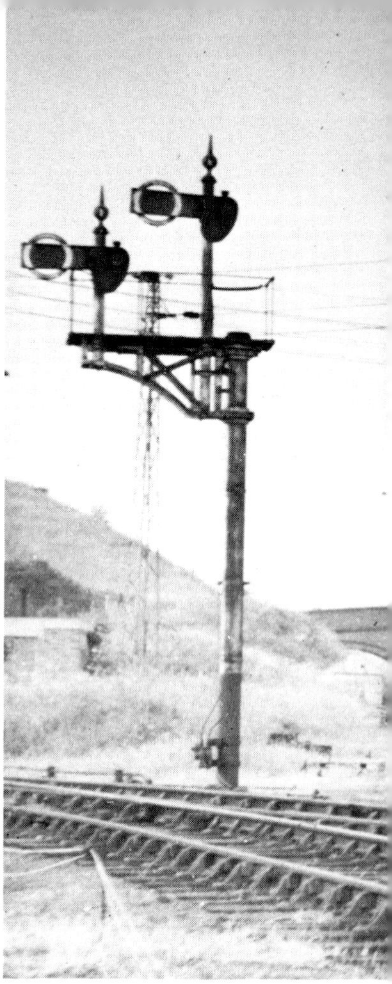

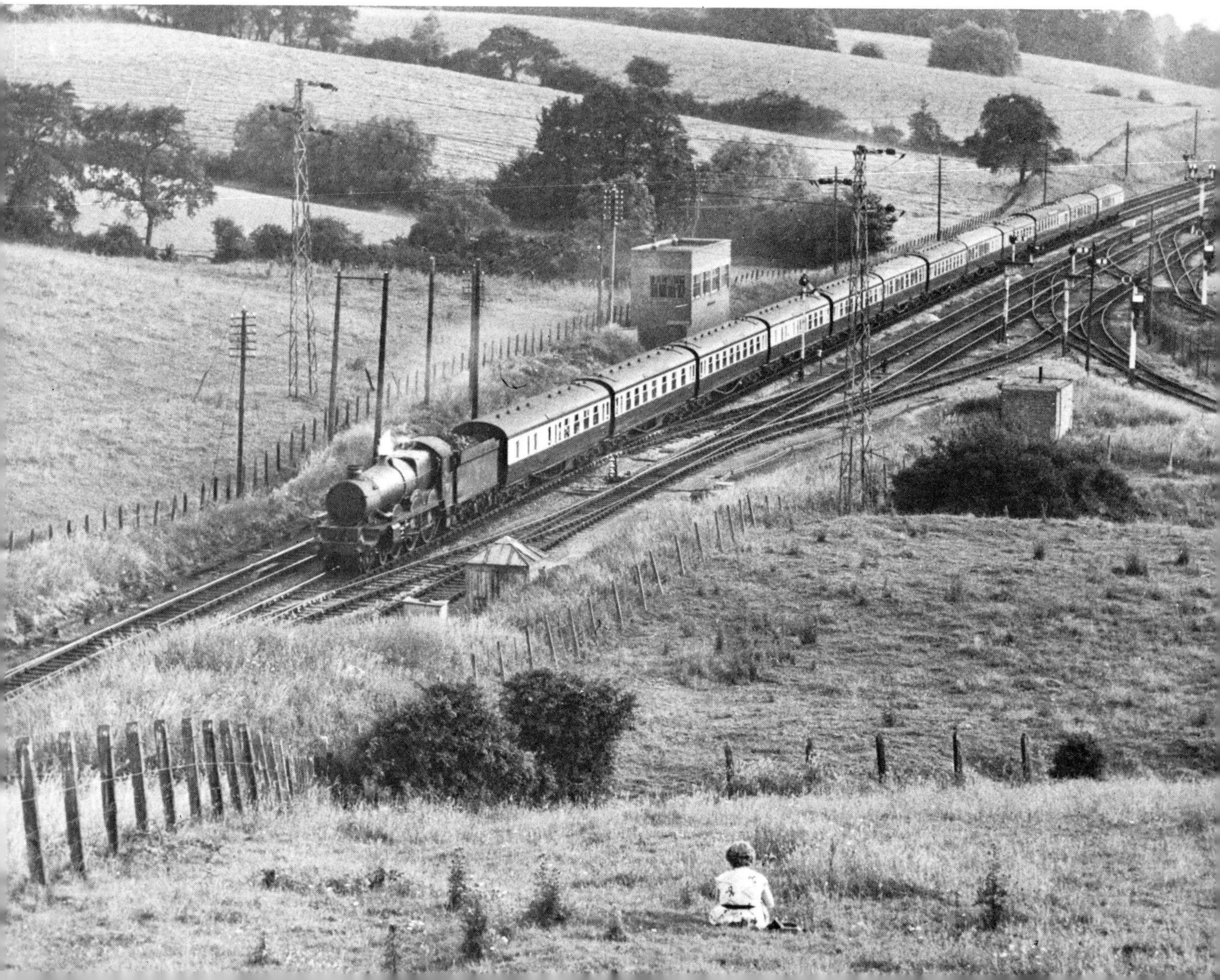

Above left: The evening meal is being served aboard the westbound 'Red Dragon' as it makes its stop at Badminton station.

Left: A South Wales-Paddington express passes Wapley Common sidings behind a 'Castle' 4-6-0 on 17 July 1955.

Above: The westbound 'Red Dragon' thunders past Wapley Common sidings with Class 7 Pacific No 70029 *Shooting Star* at the helm in July 1955.

Right: The westbound 'Pembroke Coast Express' speeds through Badminton past a WR 2-6-0 on a goods train waiting in the loop.

Above: WR 4-6-0 No 1005 *County of Devon* waiting at Chipping Sodbury with the 11.44am Swindon-Bristol stopping train for the 'Pembroke Coast Express' to overtake on the down main on 31 March 1955.

Above right: 'Britannia' Pacific No 70025 *Western Star* pauses at Badminton station with the down 'Red Dragon'.

Right: 'Britannia' Pacific No 70028 *Royal Star* approaching Chipping Sodbury with a Pembroke Dock-Paddington express.

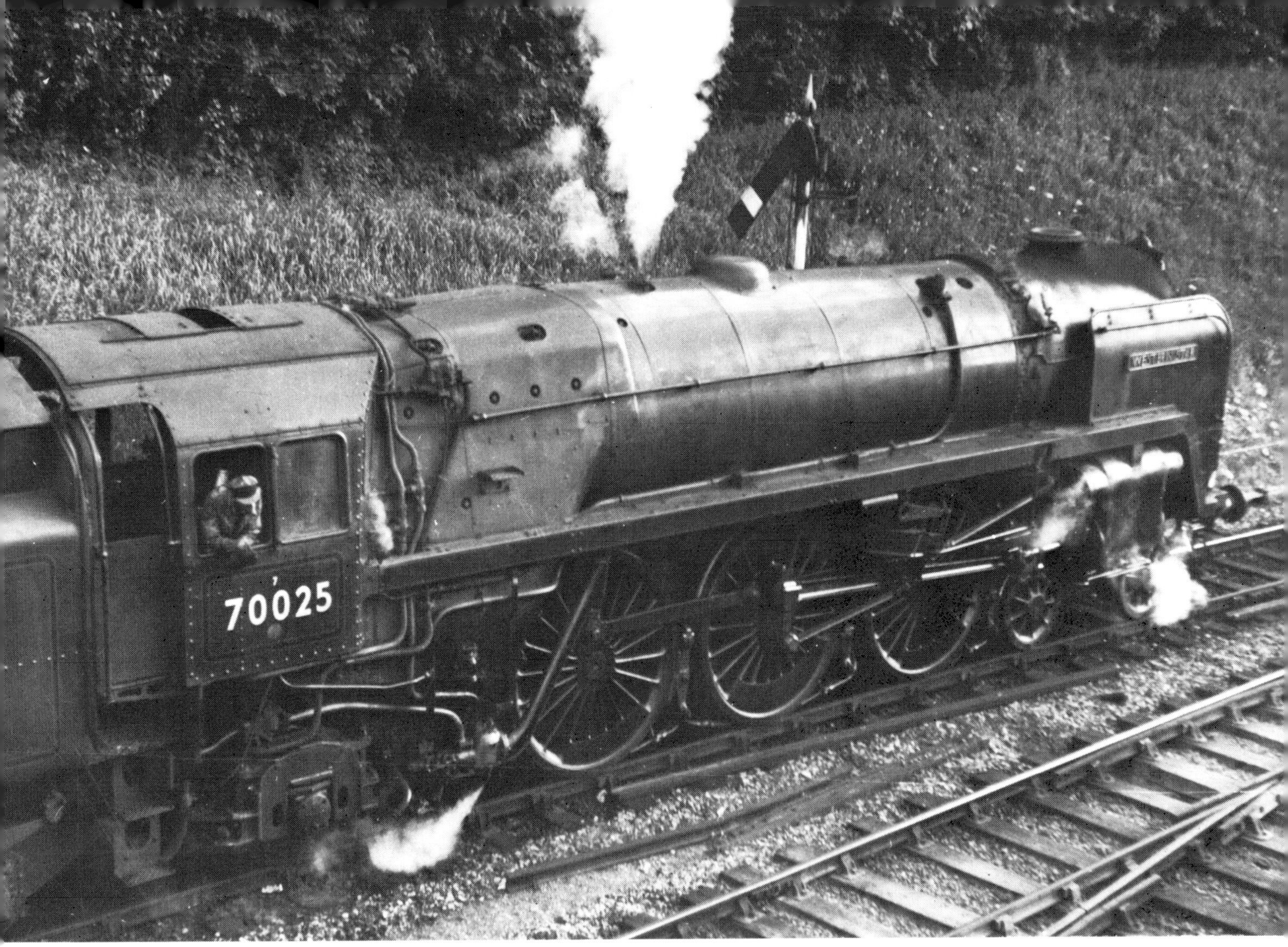
70025

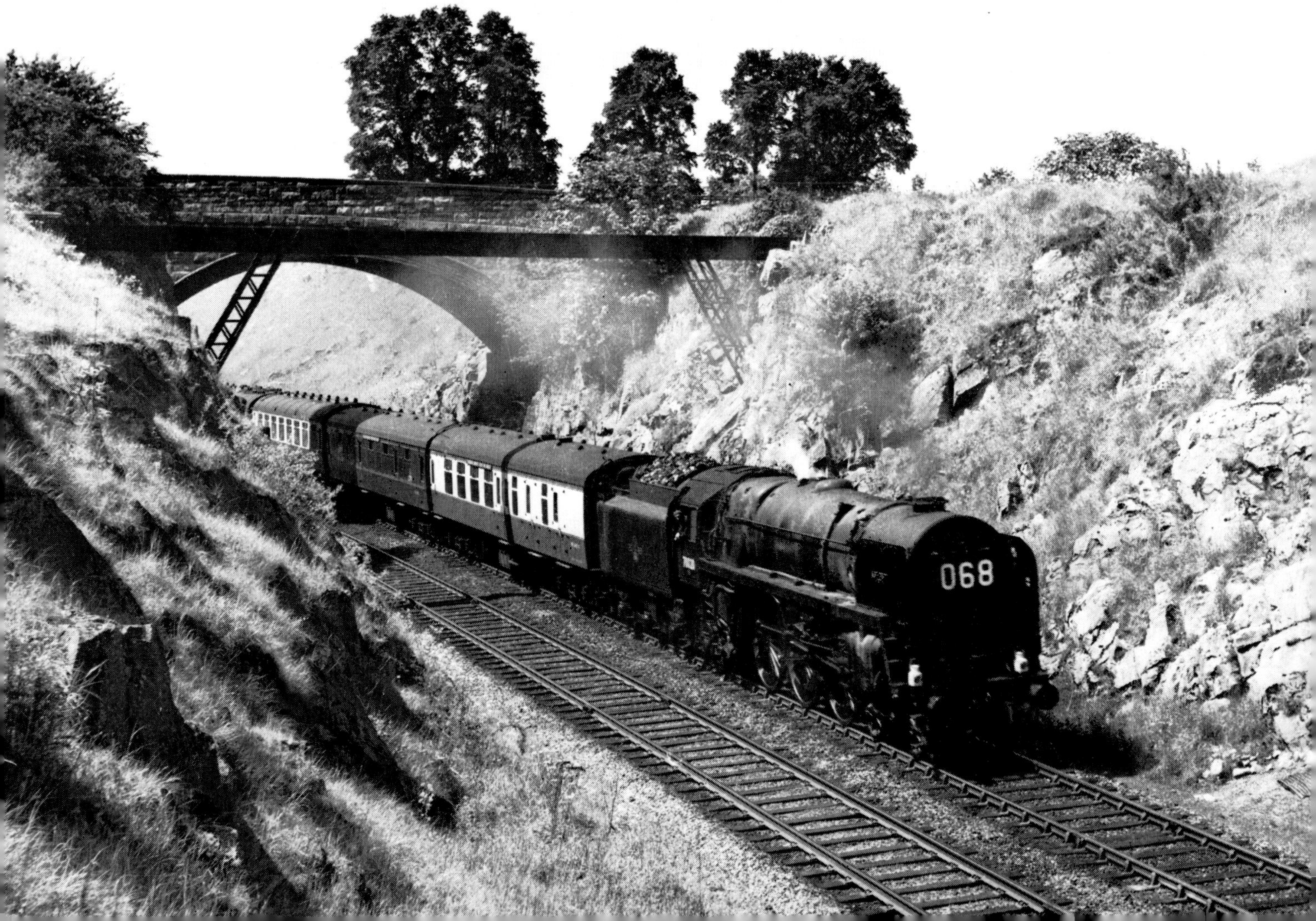
068

Above: No 5012 *Berry Pomeroy Castle* climbing through Wapley with the up 'South Wales Pullman'.

Below: No 4096 *Highclere Castle* at Wapley with the up 'Pembroke Coast Express'.

Above: The 11.45am Bristol-Paddington non-stop express thunders through Chipping Sodbury station behind a 4-6-0 in 1956.

Below: Class 7 Pacific No 70025 *Western Star* entering Badminton station with the eastbound 'Red Dragon' on 19 August 1953.

Above: A Paddington-Carmarthen express enters Alderton Tunnel, east of Badminton, behind a 'Western' diesel-hydraulic.

Below: No 5096 *Bridgwater Castle* leaving Alderton Tunnel, east of Badminton, with the Sunday 1.35pm off Bristol Temple Meads on 15 March 1953.

Above: 'Britannia' Class 7 Pacific No 70028 *Royal Star* cruises east of Badminton with the 3.55pm Paddington-Neyland express in September 1953.

Below: No 6961 *Stedham Hall* with an eastbound freight near Chipping Sodbury in May 1963.

Above: 'Western' diesel-hydraulic No D1037 *Western Empress* makes the traditional stop at Badminton station in the Beaufort country, with a Sunday evening Carmarthen-Paddington express.

Below: WR 4-6-0 'Castle' class No 5076 *Gladiator* whirls a London-bound troop train round a wide curve east of Hullavington, Wilts, on Sunday 6 September 1953.

Below: Resplendent in blue and white livery, the 'South Wales Pullman' hurries down the 1 in 300 between Sodbury Tunnel and Stoke Gifford in the spring of 1967.

Above: A 'Hymek' diesel-hydraulic at the Badminton stop with a Swansea-Paddington express in the 1960s.

Above: No 5943 *Elmdon Hall* moves a heavy freight up the embankment from Stoke Gifford yards in a freezing north wind in January 1962.

Above right: Under a cloudless winter sky a 'Castle' 4-6-0 heads a Pembroke Dock-Paddington express across Westerleigh Viaduct and clatters over the junction in December 1959.

Right: The 11.45am Bristol-Paddington two-hour express passing through Badminton behind WR 4-6-0 No 5019 *Treago Castle* in September 1953.

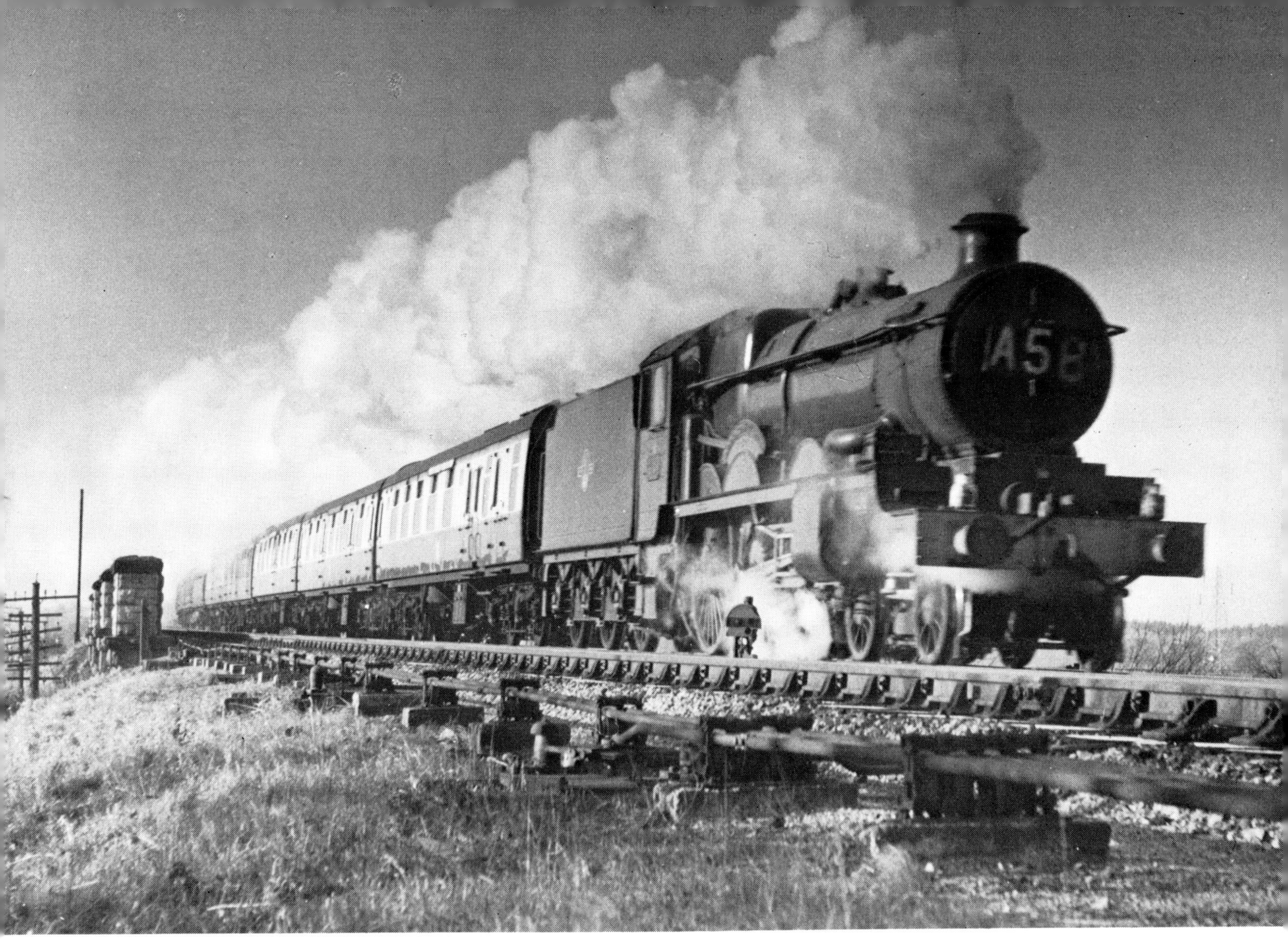

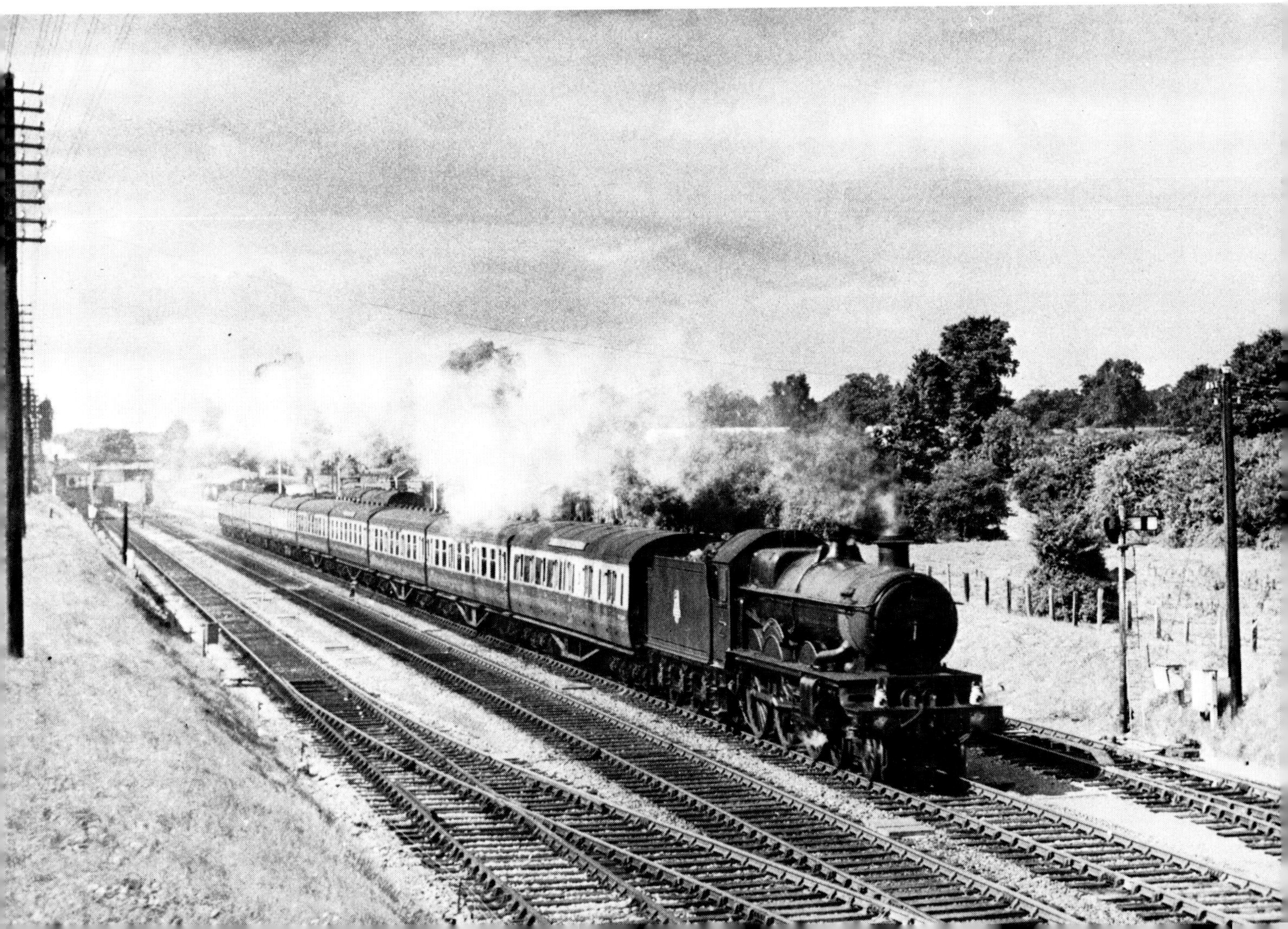

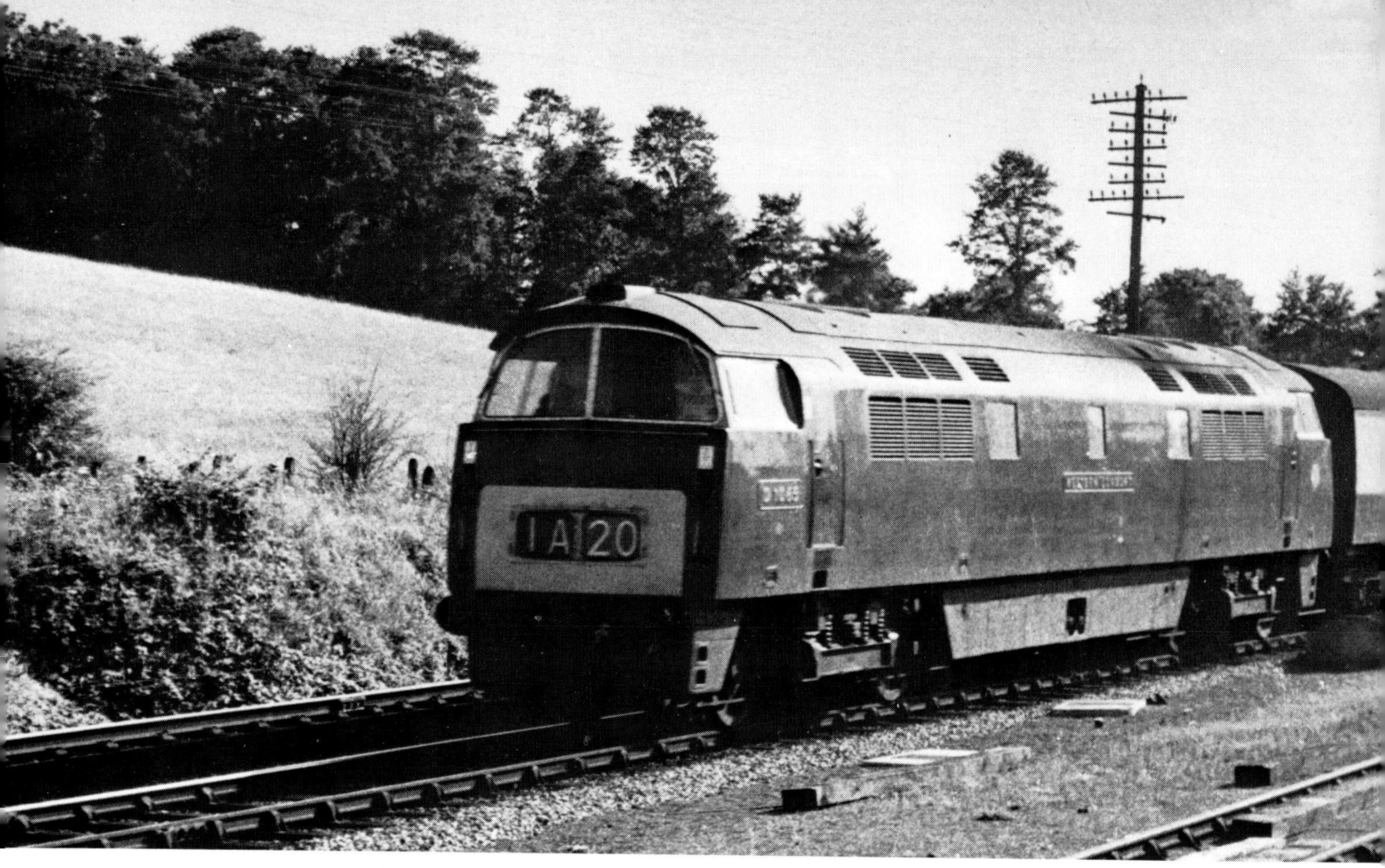
1A20

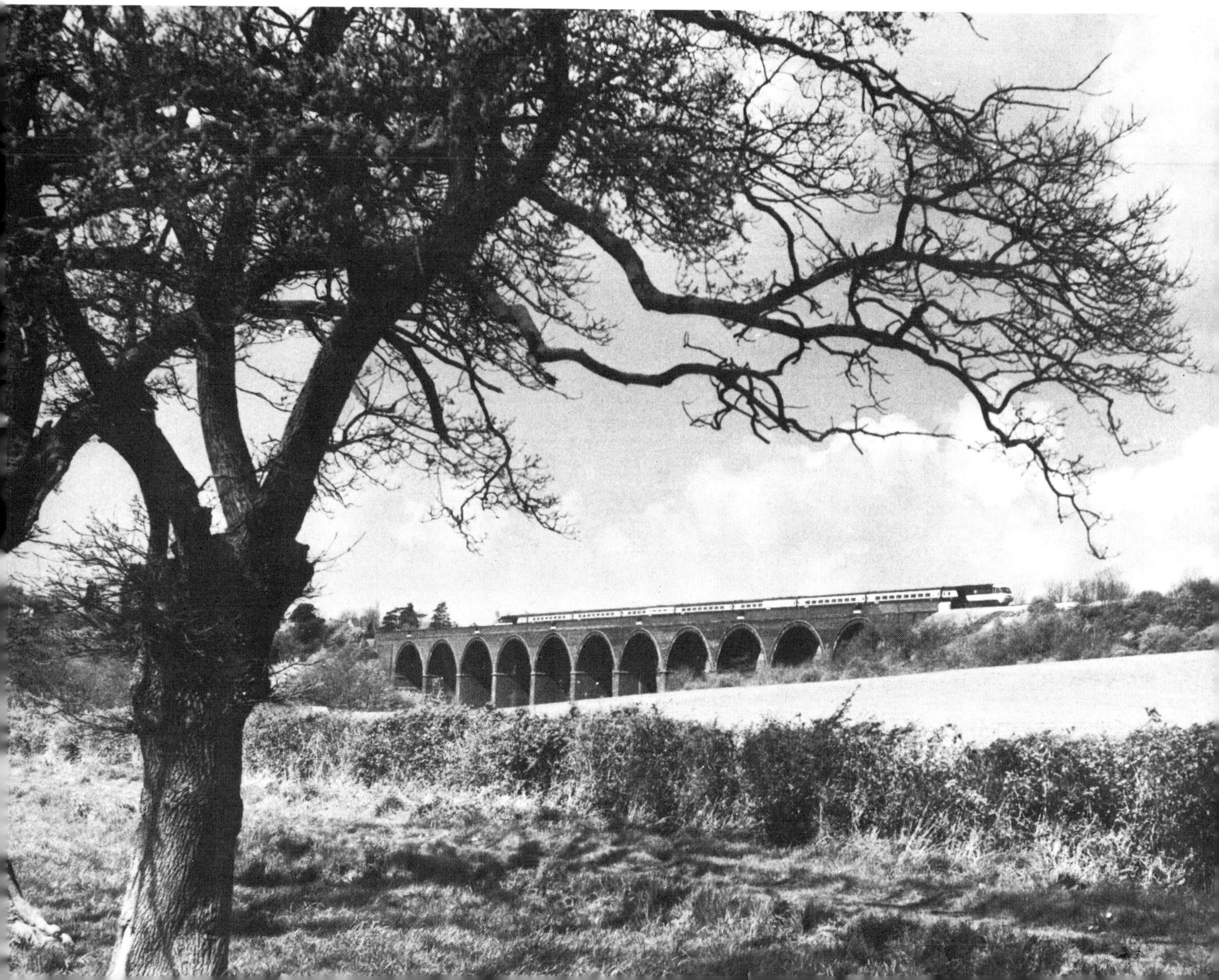

Left: 'Western' diesel-hydraulic No D1065 *Western Consort* roars up the 1 in 300 past Wapley sidings near Chipping Sodbury with a Carmarthen-Paddington express in June 1964.

Below left: A London-bound HST crossing Winterbourne Viaduct east of Bristol Parkway.

Below: The 'South Wales Pullman' emerging from Sodbury Tunnel in March 1968.

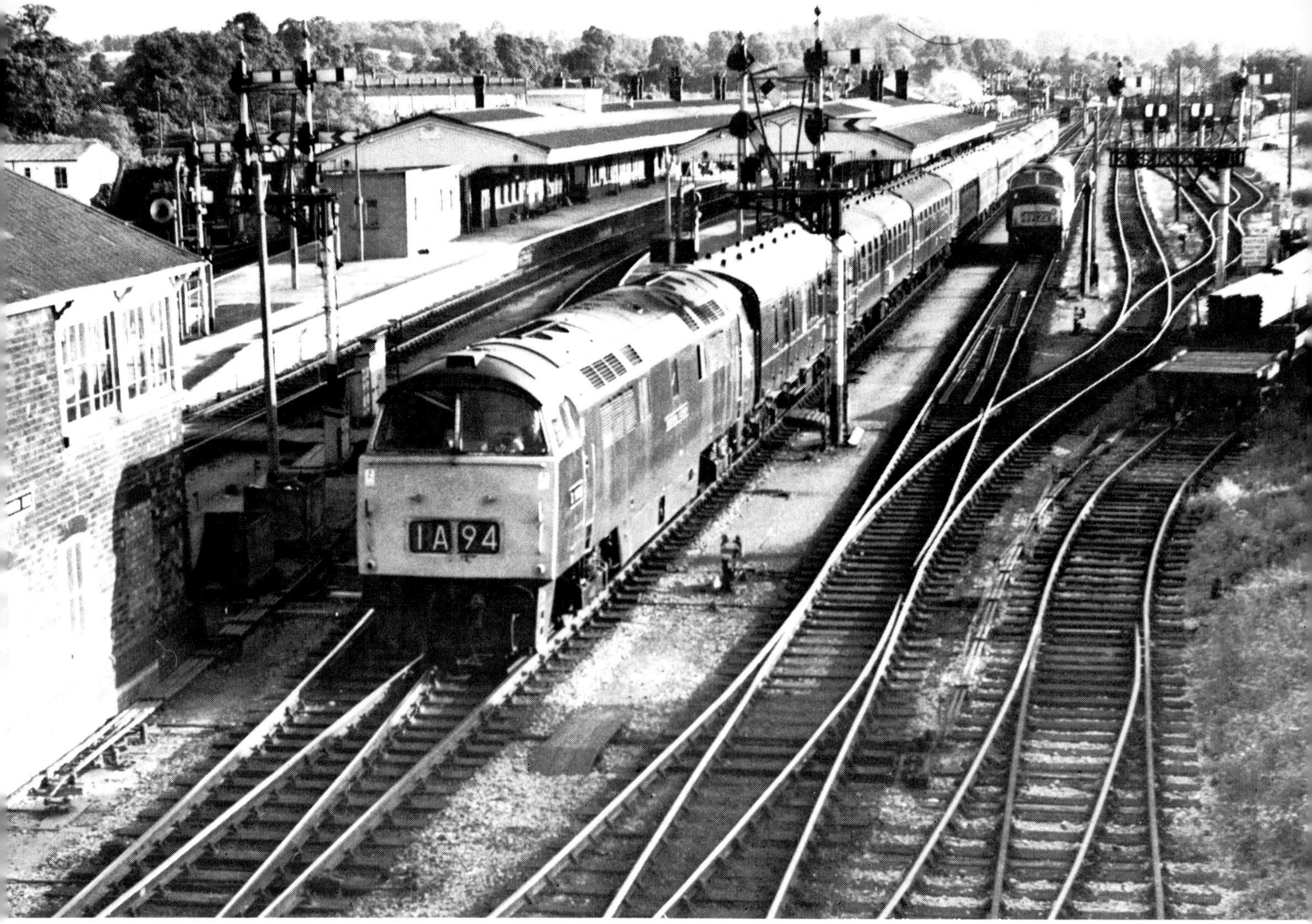
1A94

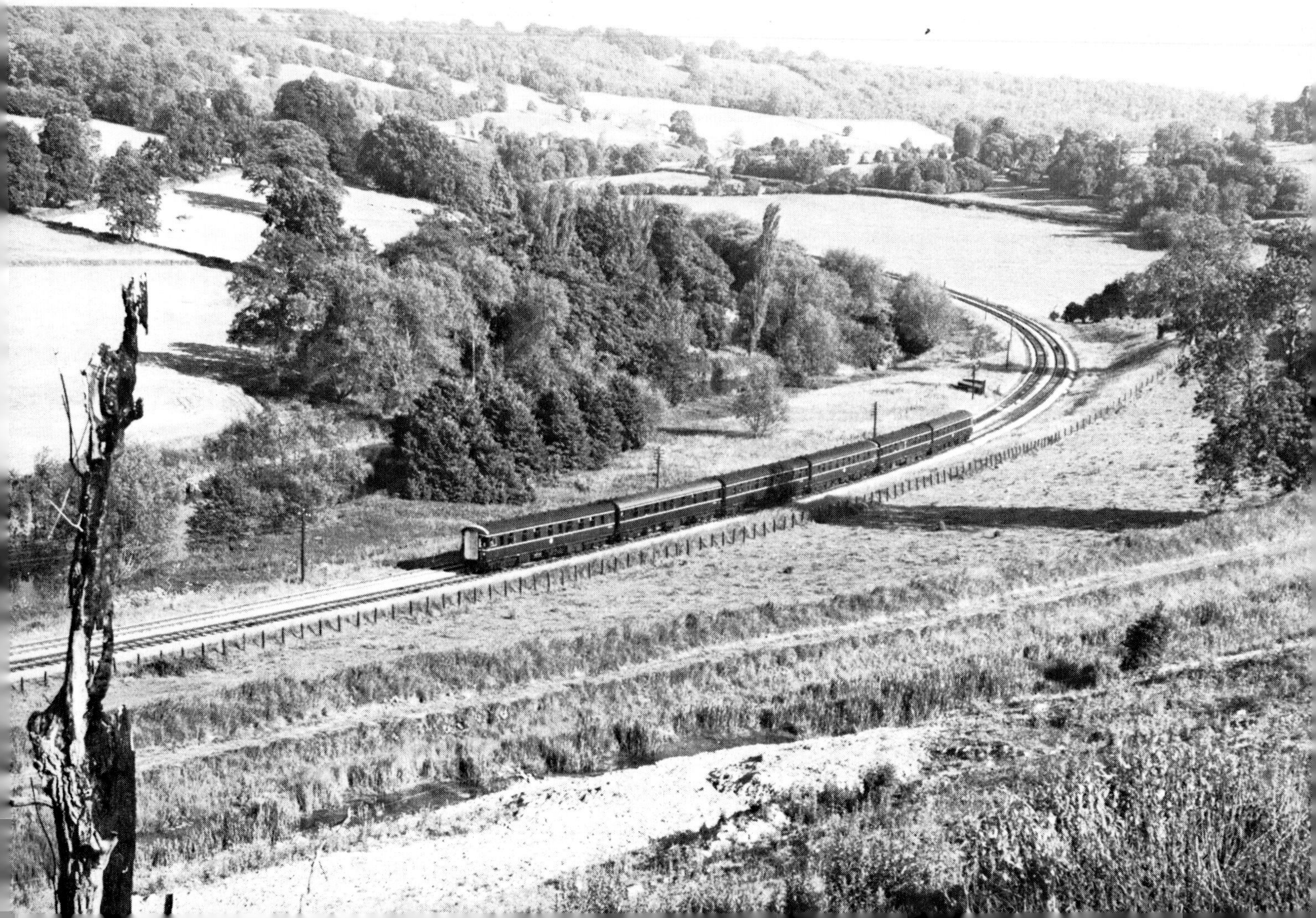

Above left: The 2.00pm Penzance-Paddington express at Westbury station in June 1967 headed by a 'Western' diesel-hydraulic.

Far left: A Cardiff-Portsmouth dmu glides gently through the picturesque Limpley Stoke Valley near Bath.

Above: 'Western' diesel-hydraulic No D1012 *Western Firebrand* roars through Badminton station with a Pembroke Dock-Paddington express in August 1963.

Left: The 2.15pm Bristol-Paddington thunders east near Corsham behind a 'Warship' diesel-hydraulic in September 1962.

49

Left: Mellow October sunshine highlights a Cardiff-Paddington Inter-City 125 as it approaches Winterbourne cutting.

Above: In clear December sunshine and a sprinkling of snow, a Cardiff-Paddington Inter-City 125 streaks through Coalpit Heath on newly relaid track.

Below: 'Western' diesel-hydraulics Nos D1023 *Western Fusilier* and D1013 *Western Ranger* emerge from Chipping Sodbury Tunnel with the 'Western Tribute' special on Saturday 26 February 1977.

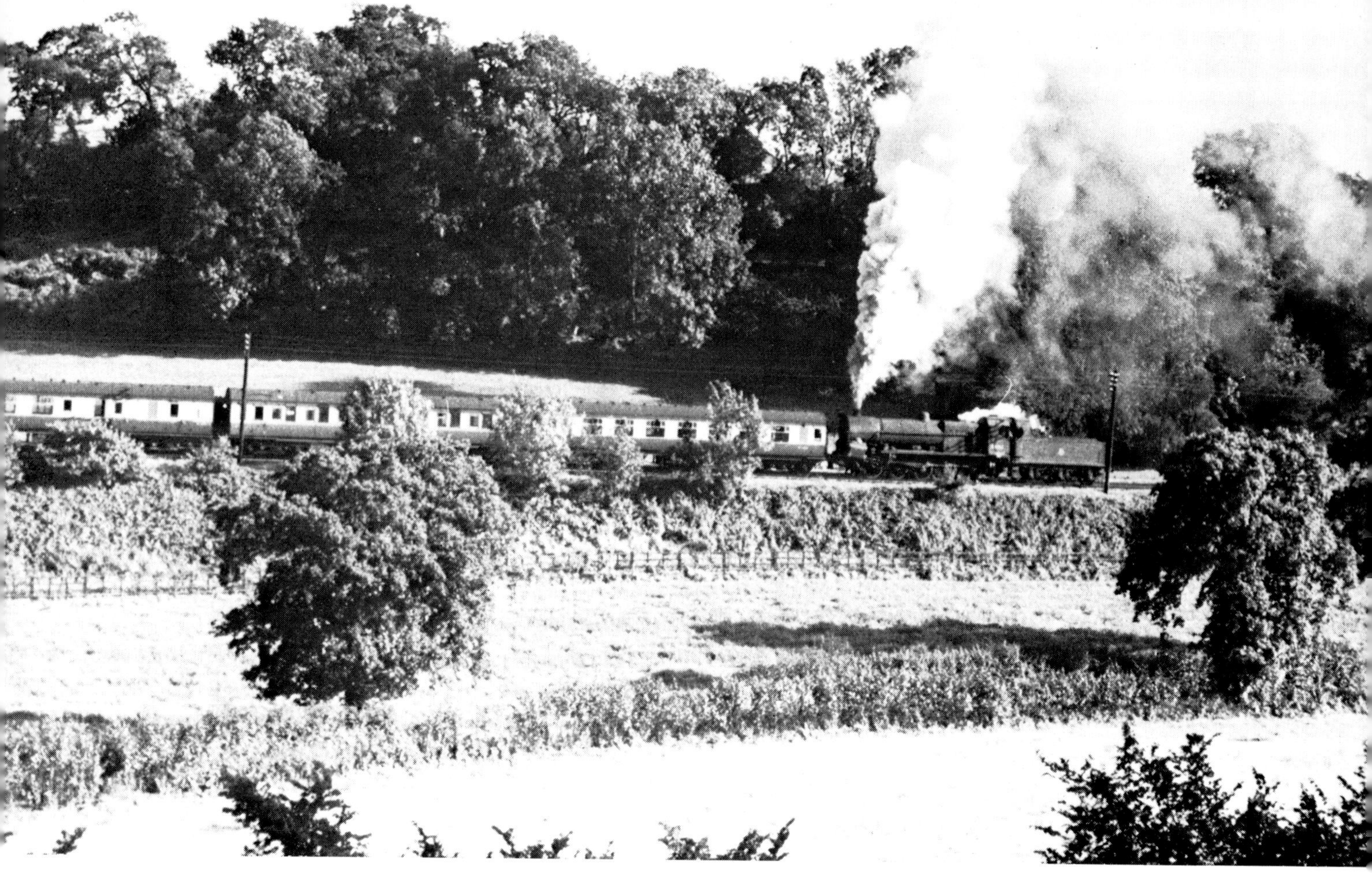

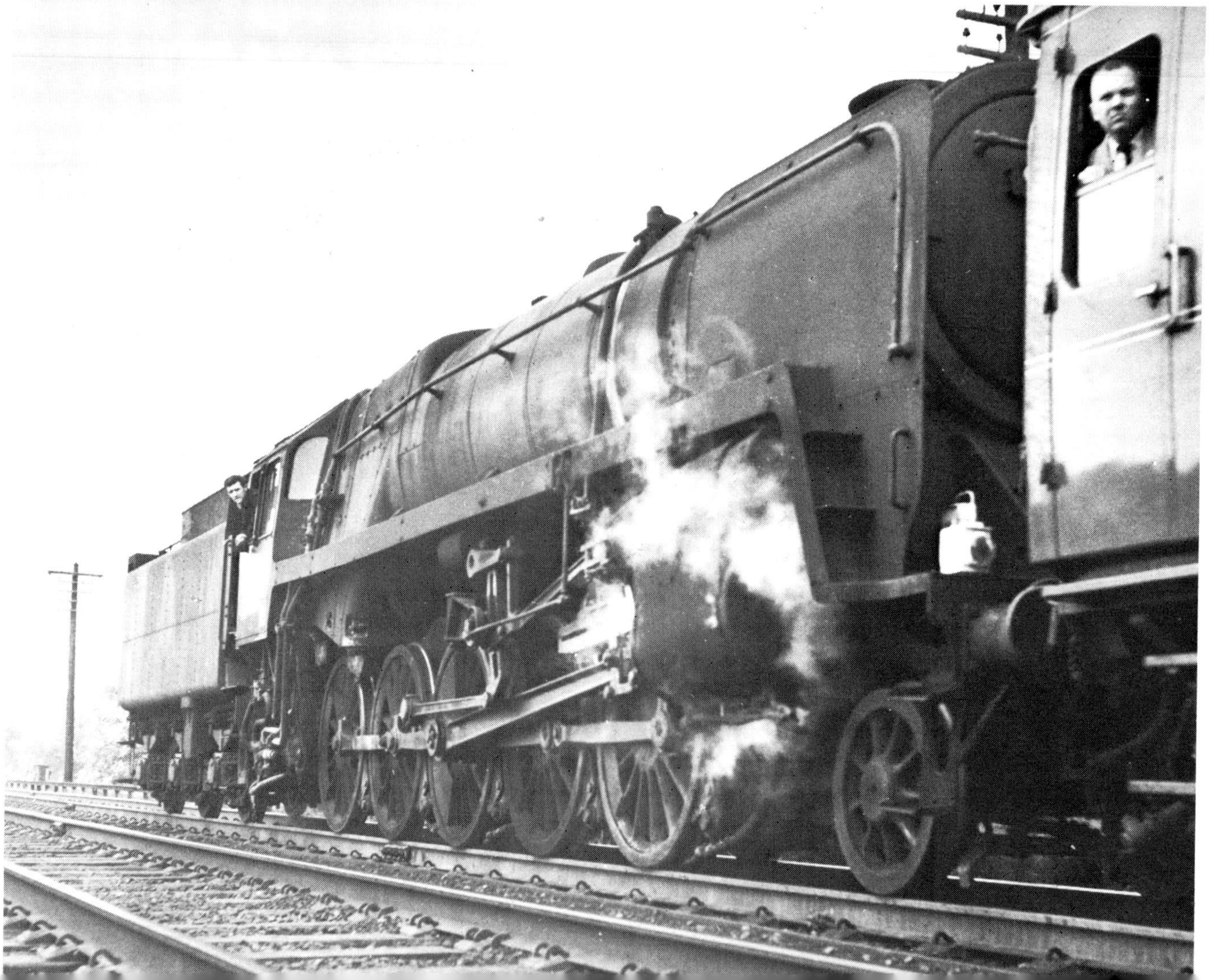

Far left: The former Midland Railway 0-10-0 banking locomotive No 58100, nicknamed 'Big Bertha', pushes hard on the tail of a northbound express up the Lickey Incline from Bromsgrove in the 1950s.

Below left: Class 9 2-10-0 No 92075 assisting a Bristol-Bradford express up the Lickey Incline in the 1960s.

Left: In complete contrast to the days of steam power, the diesels make light work of the Lickey Incline. Here a Class 46 breasts the summit unaided with a 12-coach express for Birmingham.

Below: Cumulus floats in the summer sky as a Class 46 diesel-electric lifts a 13-coach Bristol-Birmingham express up Bromsgrove Bank.

Left: No 7818 *Granville Manor* coasts under the WR viaduct at Westerleigh with a Bristol-bound freight on the main line from Birmingham.

Below: The northbound 'Cornishman' at speed near Wickwar, Glos, behind a 'Castle' 4-6-0 in July 1955.

Right: A Stanier Class 5 heads north on manicured ballast at Westerleigh with a Bristol-Gloucester all-stations train in the 1950s.

Right: Late in the evening, south of Wickwar, a Newcastle-Bristol express nears the end of its journey behind Class 5 4-6-0 No 45253 in June 1954.

Below: Laying ballast on new track at Rangeworthy, on the Bristol-North of England main line on 6 March 1955.

Below right: The last of the passenger expresses have passed and there will be no more for some hours now, so Class 4F 0-6-0 No 44035 gets the road for an uninterrupted run past Wickwar south to Bristol with a heavy coal drag in June 1954.

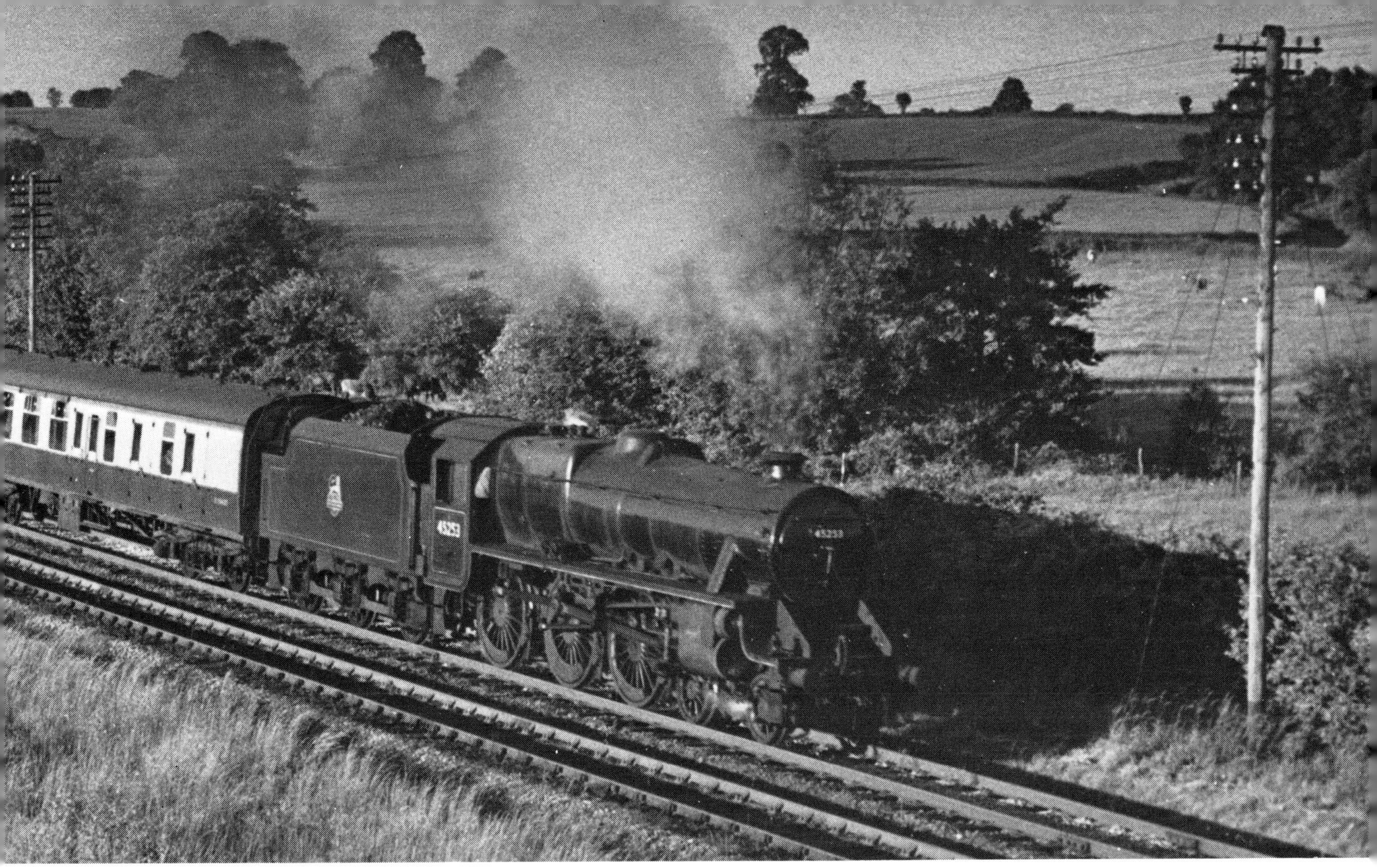

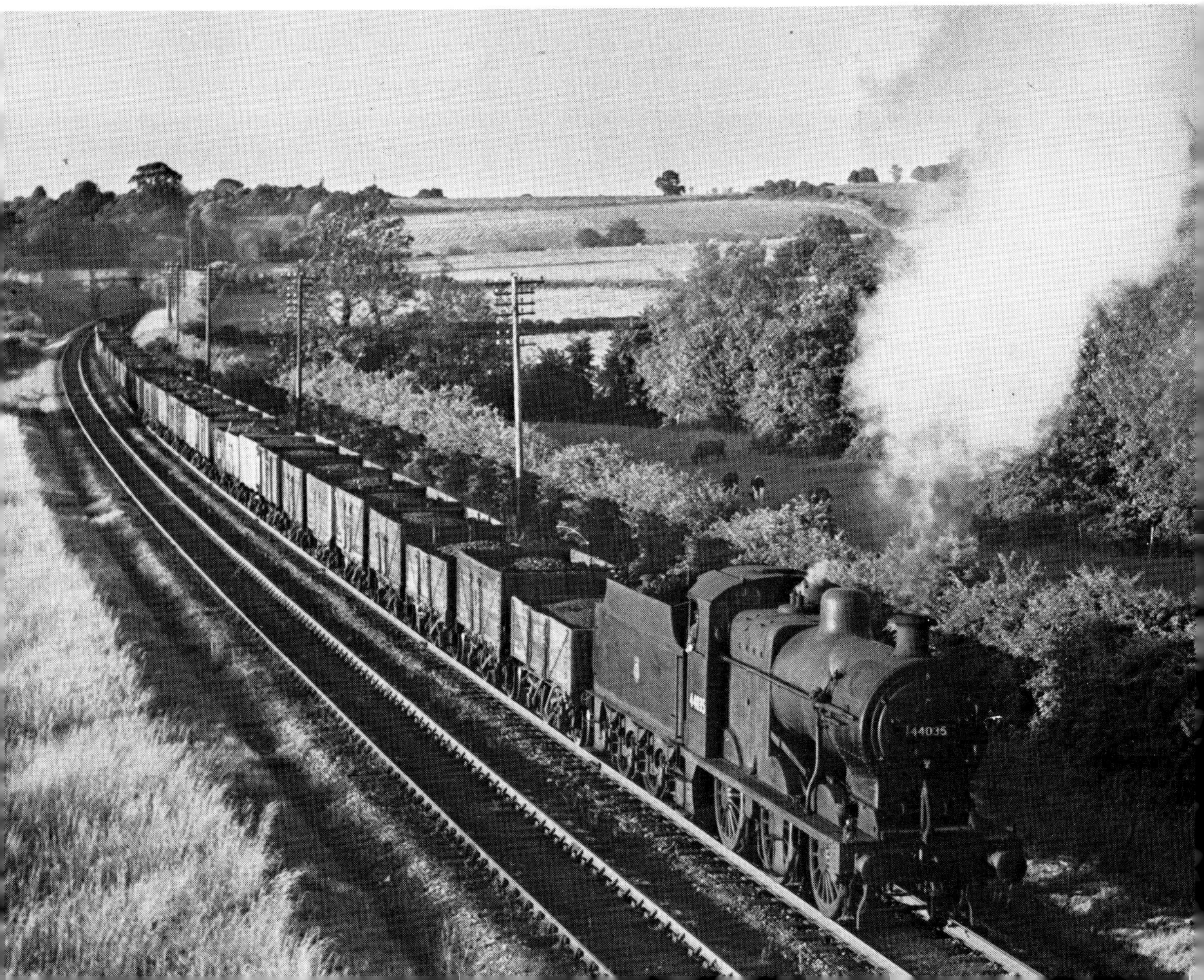
44035

BARTON STREET JUNCTION

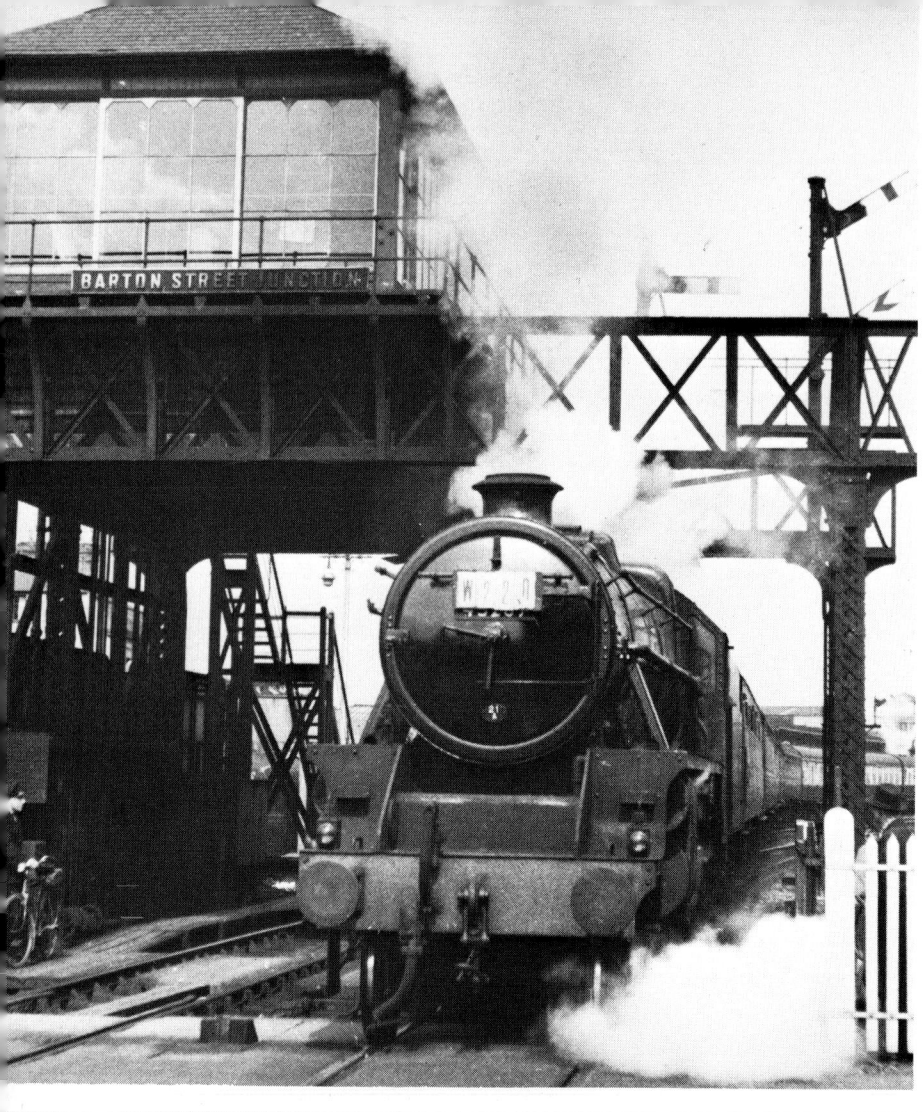

Left: Stanier 'Black Five' No 45287 storms out of Gloucester Eastgate across Barton Street crossing with a Bradford-Bristol express.

Below: Stanier Class 5 4-6-0 No 44804 at Gloucester Eastgate with the northbound 'Pines Express' on 25 August 1956.

Right: In immaculate condition, 'Jubilee' class 4-6-0 No 45662 *Kempenfelt* leaves Wickwar Tunnel with the 'Devonian' Paignton-Bradford express.

Below right: The confines of the steep cutting echo to the throaty roar of Stanier's 5XP 'Jubilee' class No 45572 *Eire*, as the 4-6-0 enters Wickwar Tunnel with a Newcastle-Bristol express.

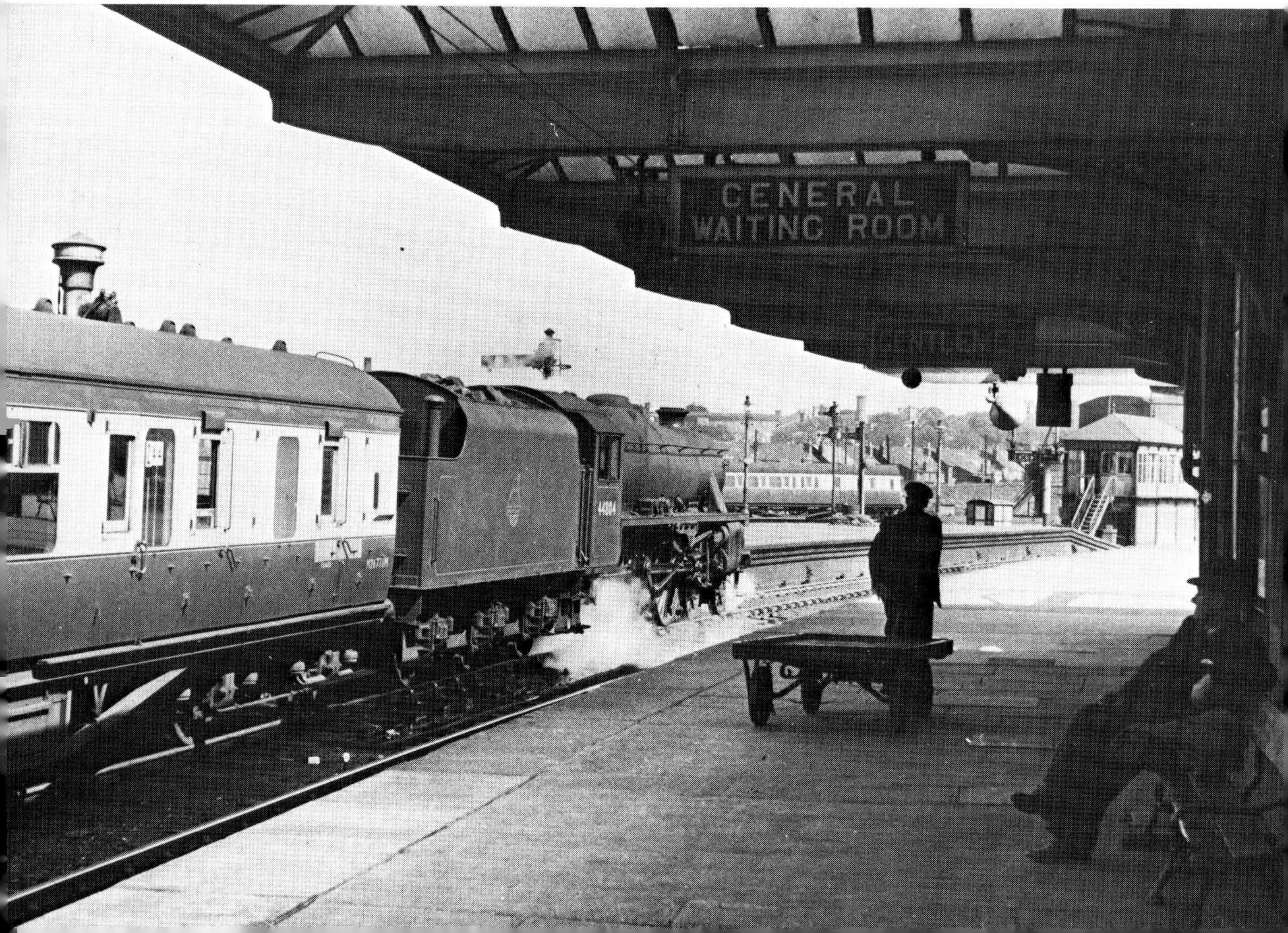
GENERAL
WAITING ROOM

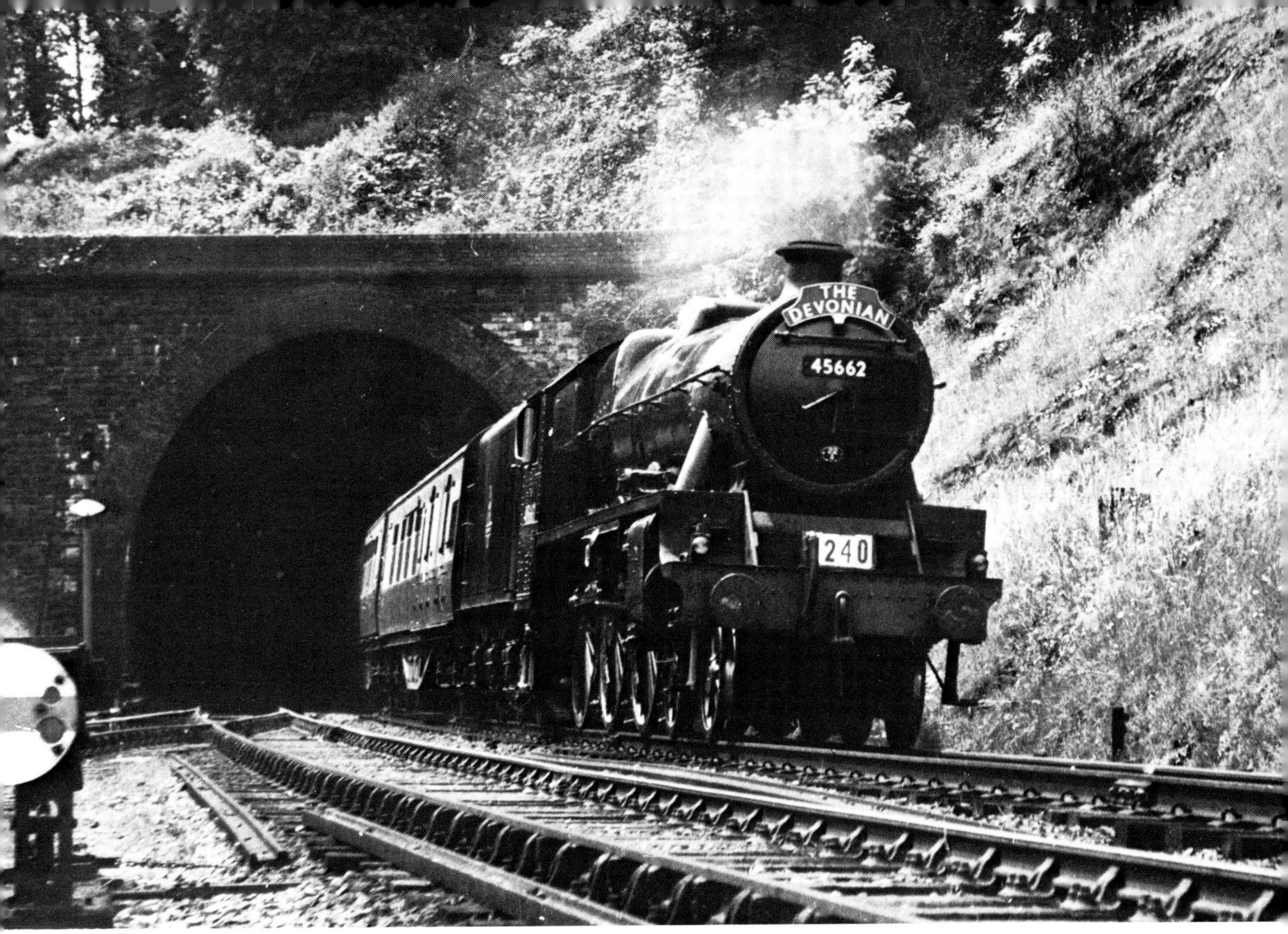
THE
DEVONIAN
45662
240

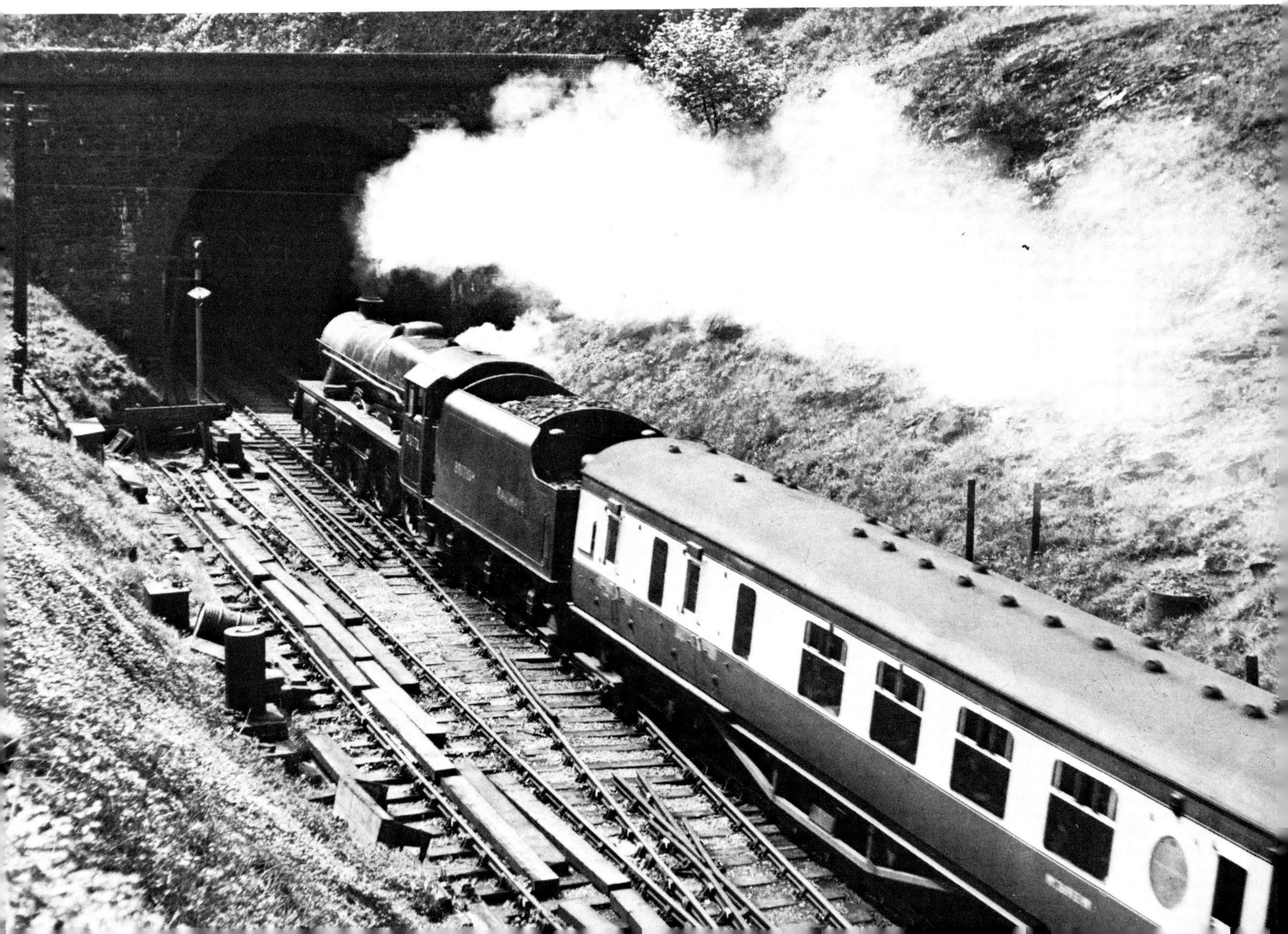

Above: 'Jubilee' 4-6-0 No 45612 *Jamaica* heads south near Rangeworthy with a Newcastle–Bristol express on a bright June evening in 1961.

Below: 'Jubilee' 4-6-0 No 45631 *Tanganyika* coasts down towards Charfield with a northbound freight from Bristol in March 1964.

Above: Class 9 2-10-0 No 92248 climbing away from Charfield with a Bristol-bound freight in March 1964.

Below: At 70mph 'Patriot' class 4-6-0 No 45519 *Lady Godiva* sweeps round a bend north of Charfield (Glos) with the 12 noon Bradford-Bristol express in May 1959.

Above: Class 9 2-10-0 No 92203 rumbles westward near Westerleigh with a heavy freight for Wales.

Right: Class 9 2-10-0 No 92135 about to move northwards out of Westerleigh marshalling yards with fitted freight for the Midlands.

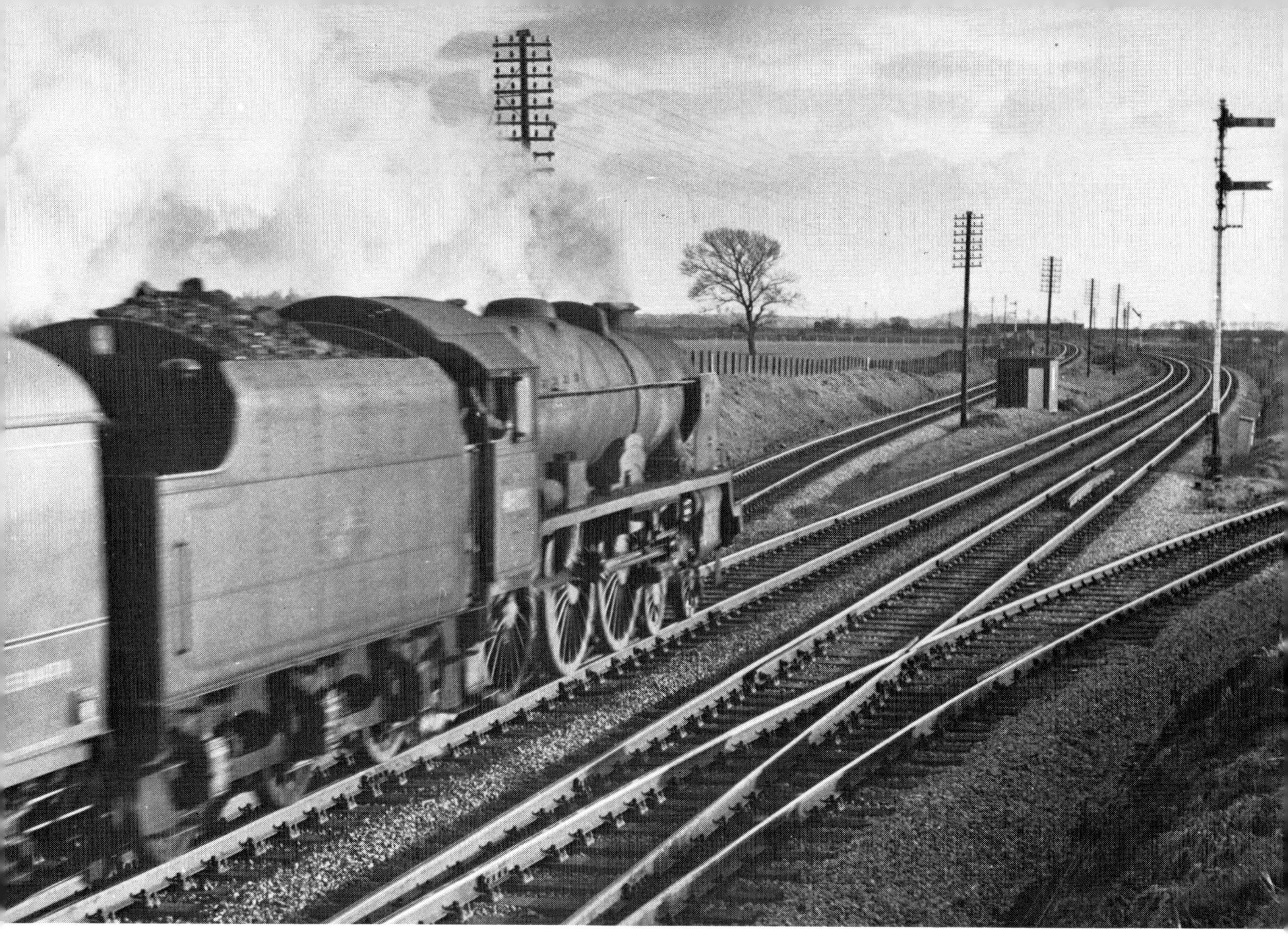

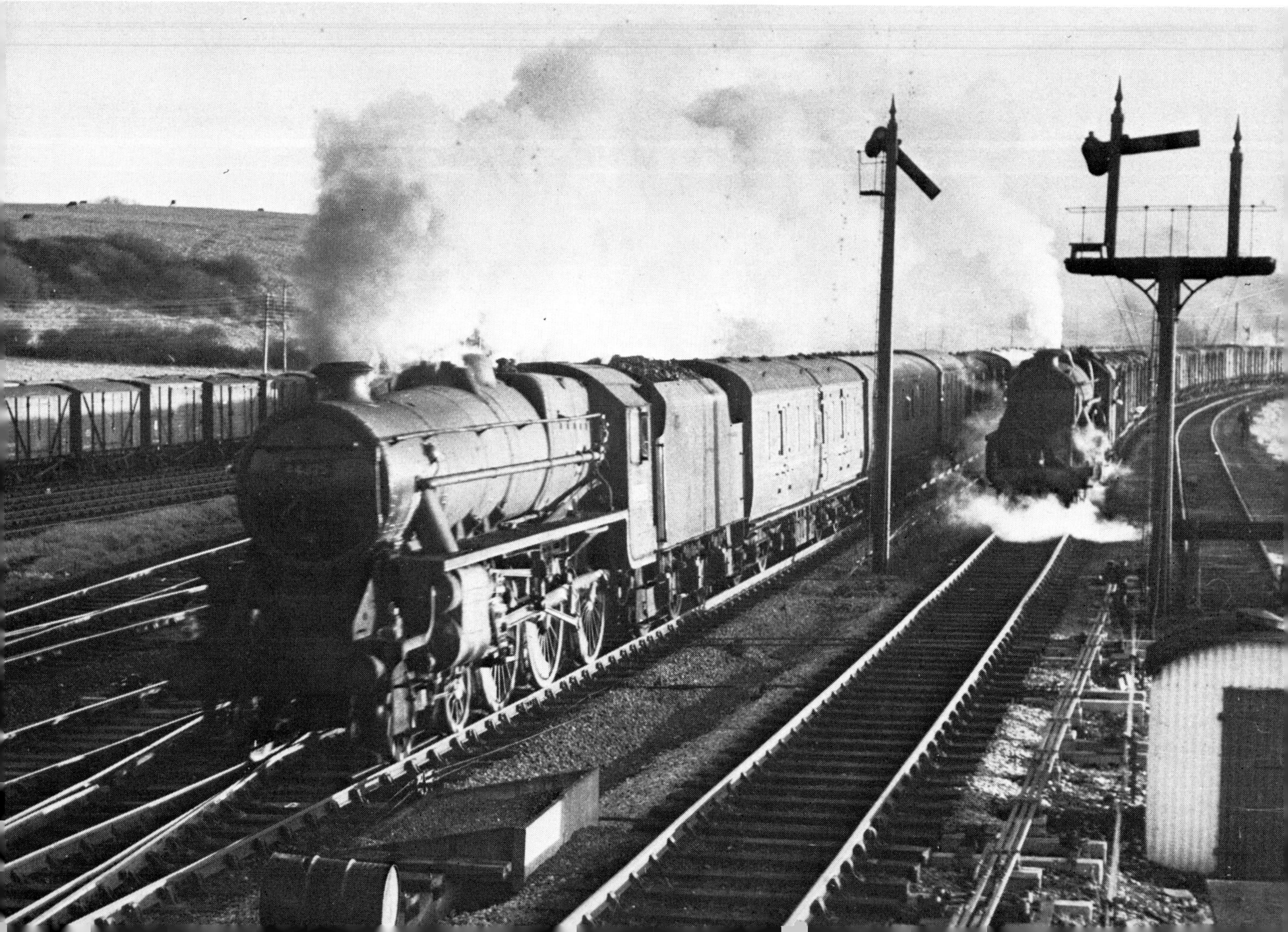

Above left: In the final days of steam power, a rebuilt 'Scot' thunders past Yate South Junction at 80mph with a Newcastle-Bristol express.

Above: No 6871 *Bourton Grange* emerges from Wickwar Tunnel with a parcels train from Birmingham to Bristol in July 1964.

Left: Stanier Class 5 No 44825 heads north through Westerleigh marshalling yards at the northern outskirts of Bristol with the 4.48pm Bristol-Leeds; the Class 5 waiting with the fitted freight will follow close behind.

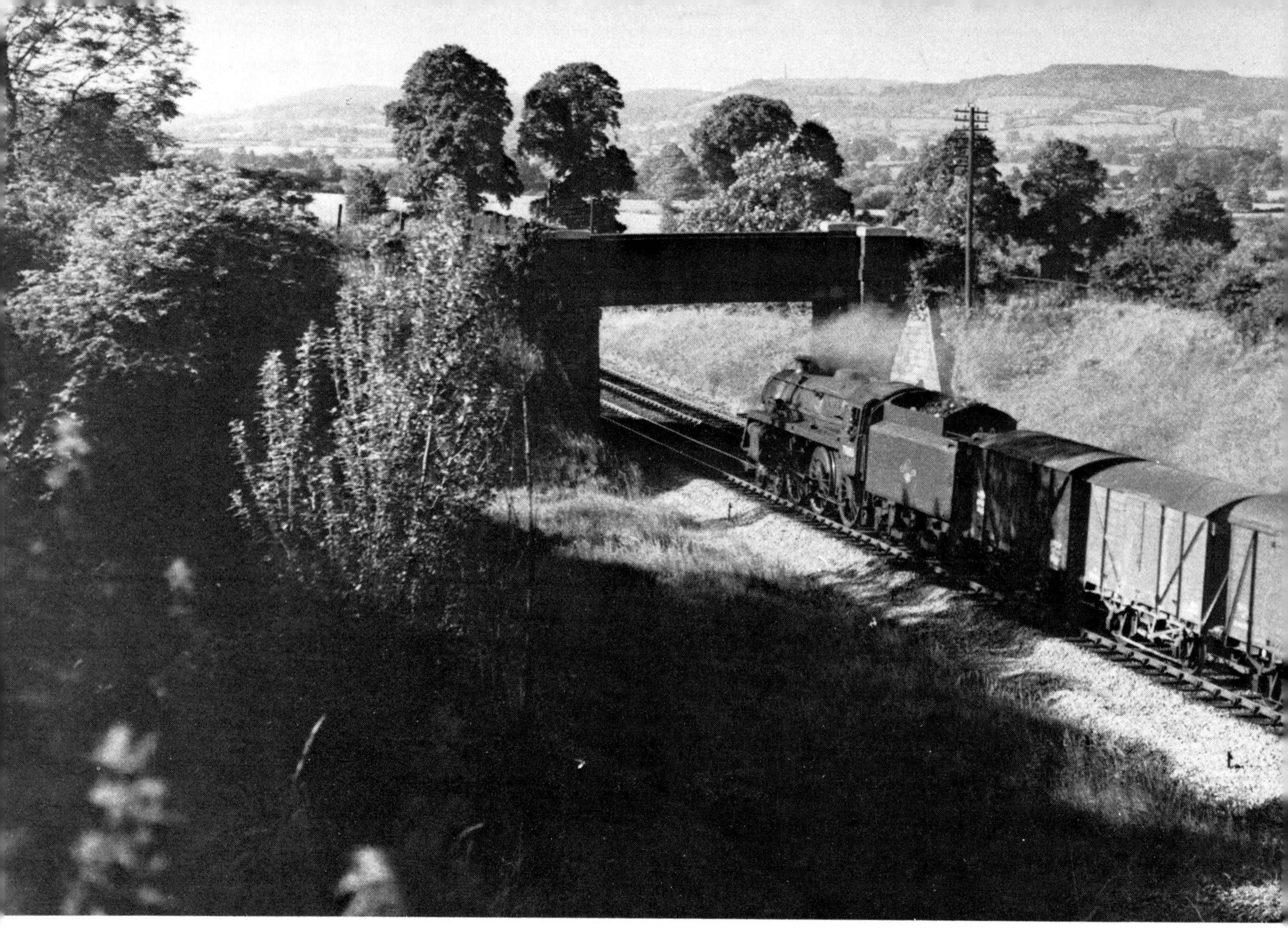

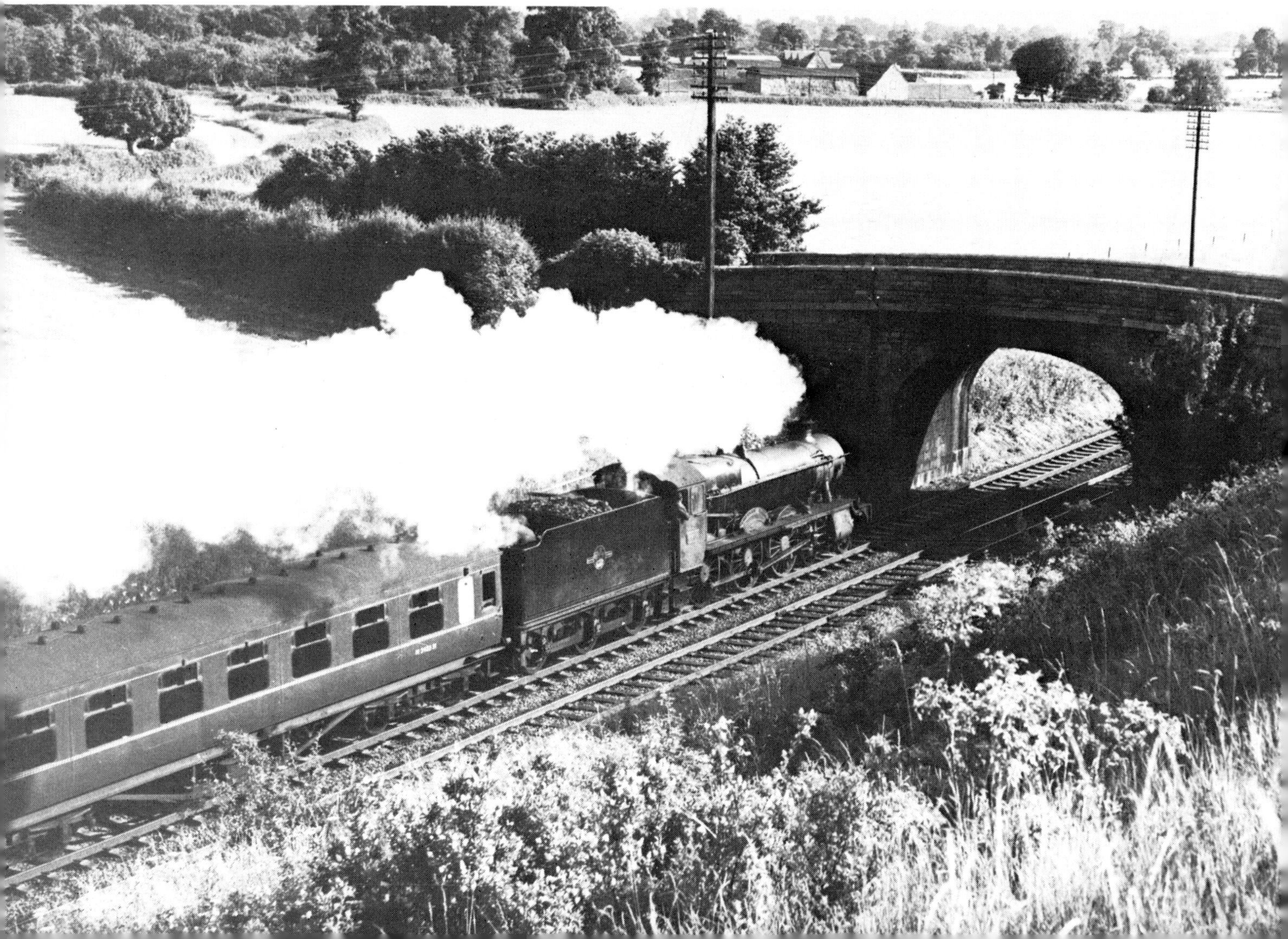

Left: The Cotswold hills provide the background to this pleasant North Gloucestershire landscape in the early 1960s. The BR Standard Class 5 4-6-0 is approaching Charfield with the regular evening fast freight from Westerleigh yards to the Midlands.

Below left: A North-to-West train heads for Bristol behind a 'Hall' class 4-6-0, seen here at Rangeworthy, soon after leaving Wickwar Tunnel.

Below: Through unspoilt Gloucestershire countryside near Charfield, a Newcastle-Bristol express runs doubleheaded by a 'Jubilee' 4-6-0 and a Fowler 2P 4-4-0. The prominent landmark in the background is North Nibley Monument on the Cotswolds.

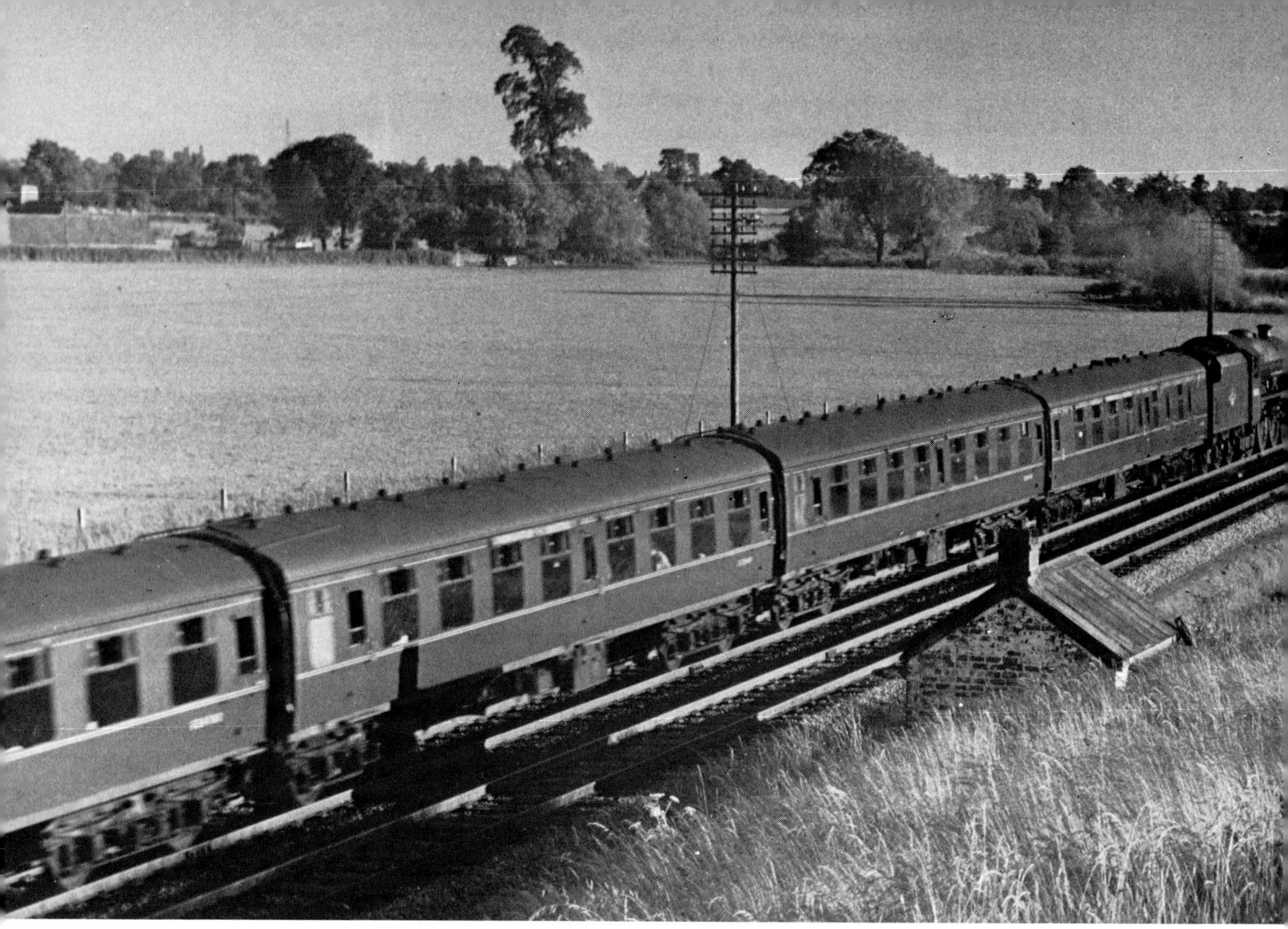

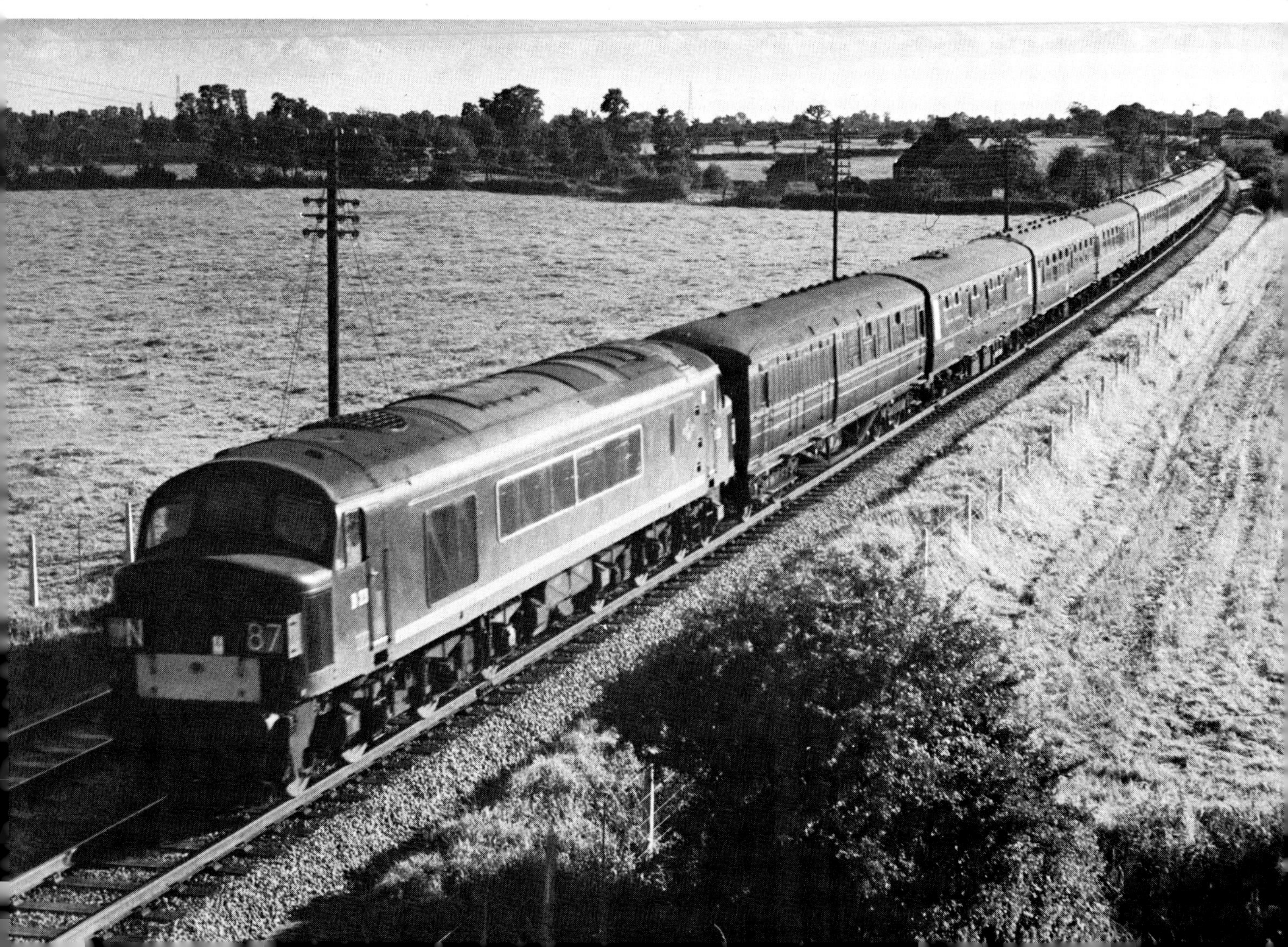

N
87

Left: An unusual sight in the last year of express steam haulage on the Bristol-North of England line was a clean 'Jubilee'; most of them were in a neglected condition externally. Here was an exception, a polished 'Jubilee' glinting in the evening sunlight on a Newcastle-Bristol express just after leaving Wickwar Tunnel in June 1961, the eve of dieselisation for this route.

Below left: Class 45 diesel-electric No D23 heads the 5.00pm Bristol-York express past Rangeworthy box, north of Yate, in September 1962.

Below: The 7.45am Bristol-Bradford express passing Westerleigh behind Class 45 diesel No D37 in the 1960s.

Right: The northbound 'Devonian' crossing Mangotsfield North Junction in October 1961, double-headed by Class 45 diesels Nos D12 and D25.

Above: 'Jubilee' 4-6-0 No 45579 *Punjab* leans to the curve at the approach to Westerleigh yards with a Newcastle-Bristol express.

Above right: In the transition period from steam to diesel traction this odd sight was not uncommon. The northbound 'Devonian', still in chocolate and cream livery, rumbles over Mangotsfield South Junction, at the summit of the long climb out of Bristol, with a Class 45 diesel piloting a 'Jubilee' 4-6-0.

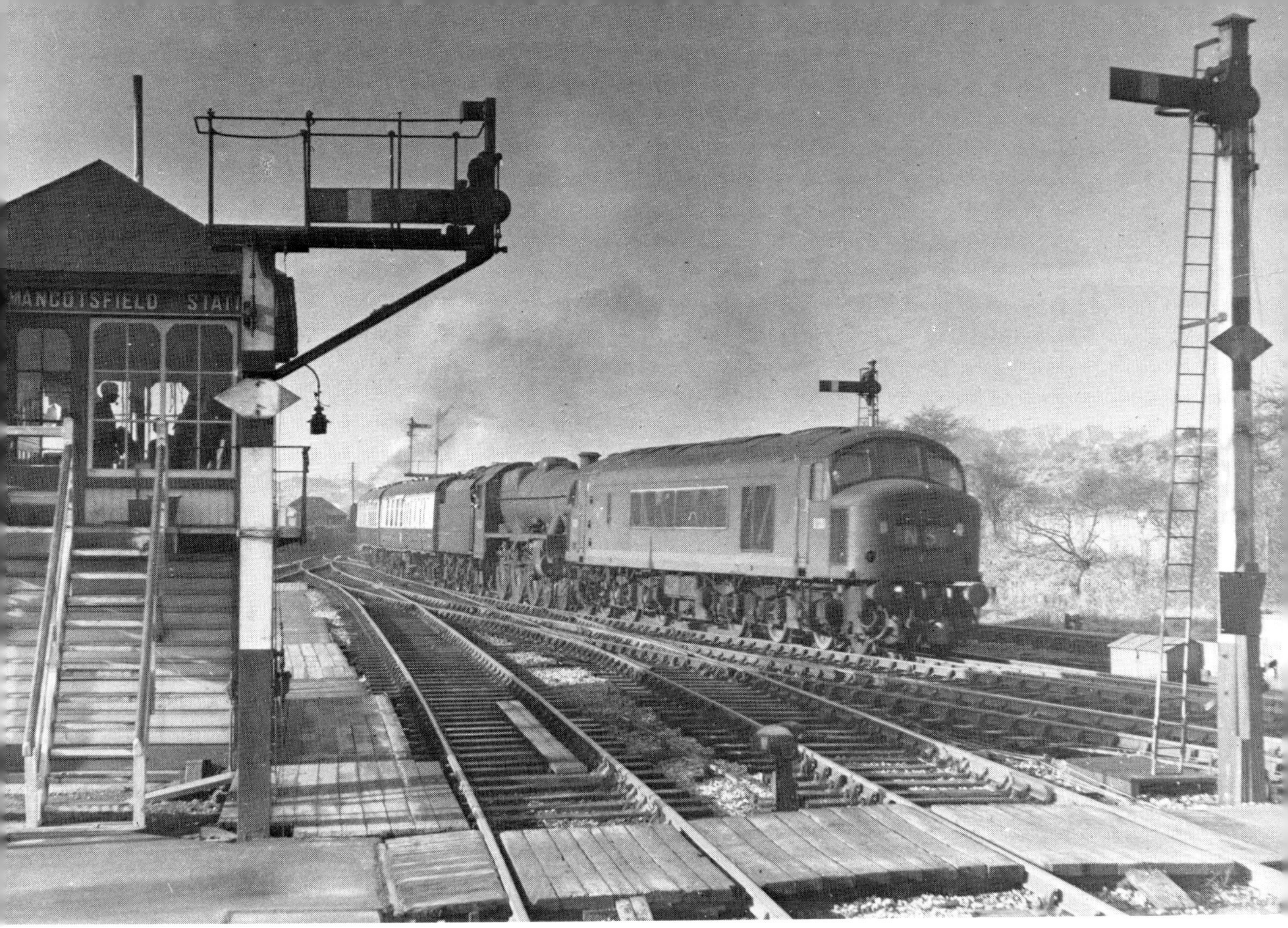
MANGOTSFIELD STAT

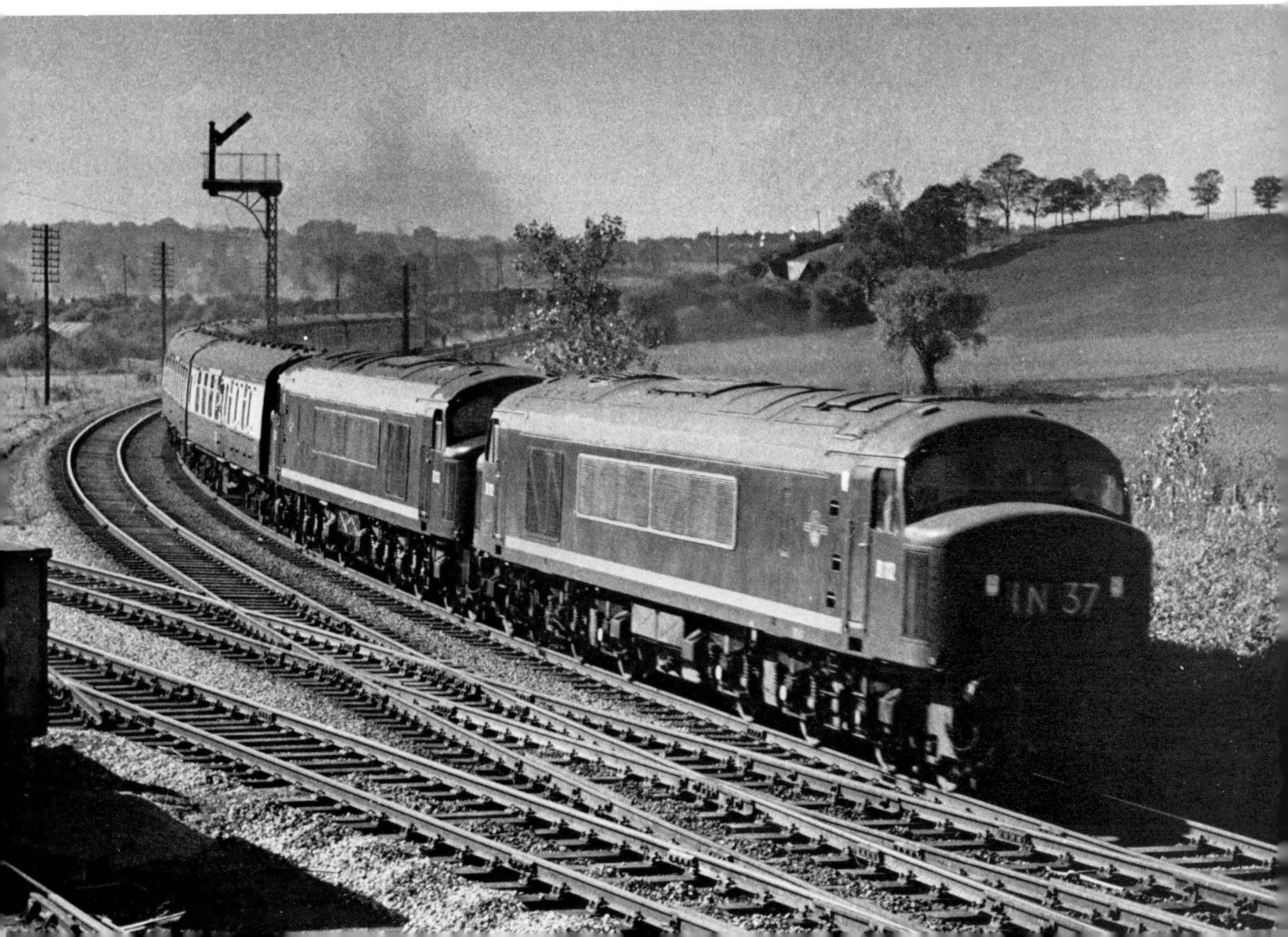
1N 37

Above: Stanier Class 5 No 44856 and 'Jubilee' No 45573 *Newfoundland* doublehead the northbound 'Devonian' through Stoke Gifford yards (now Parkway station) in the late 1950s.

Below: Class 9 2-10-0 No 92241 takes the loop from Yate Midland to Westerleigh main line with a petrol tanker train.

'Castles' storm Sapperton Bank, No 5019 *Treago Castle* leading.

'King' class 4-6-0 No 6028 *King George VI* heads the 'Torbay Express' near Twyford.

'Britannia' Pacific No 70028 *Royal Star* leaves Badminton with the 'Red Dragon'.

A 'Western' at speed.

Right: Driver and fireman of Class 5 4-6-0 No 44943 chat while waiting for the 5.00pm Bristol-York express to pass through Westerleigh yards on the up main, after which they will move out with a fast freight to the Midlands.

Below: A West to North of England excursion headed by a 'Hall' 4-6-0 joining the Bristol-Birmingham main line at Yate after coming off the South Wales main line at Westerleigh in June 1962.

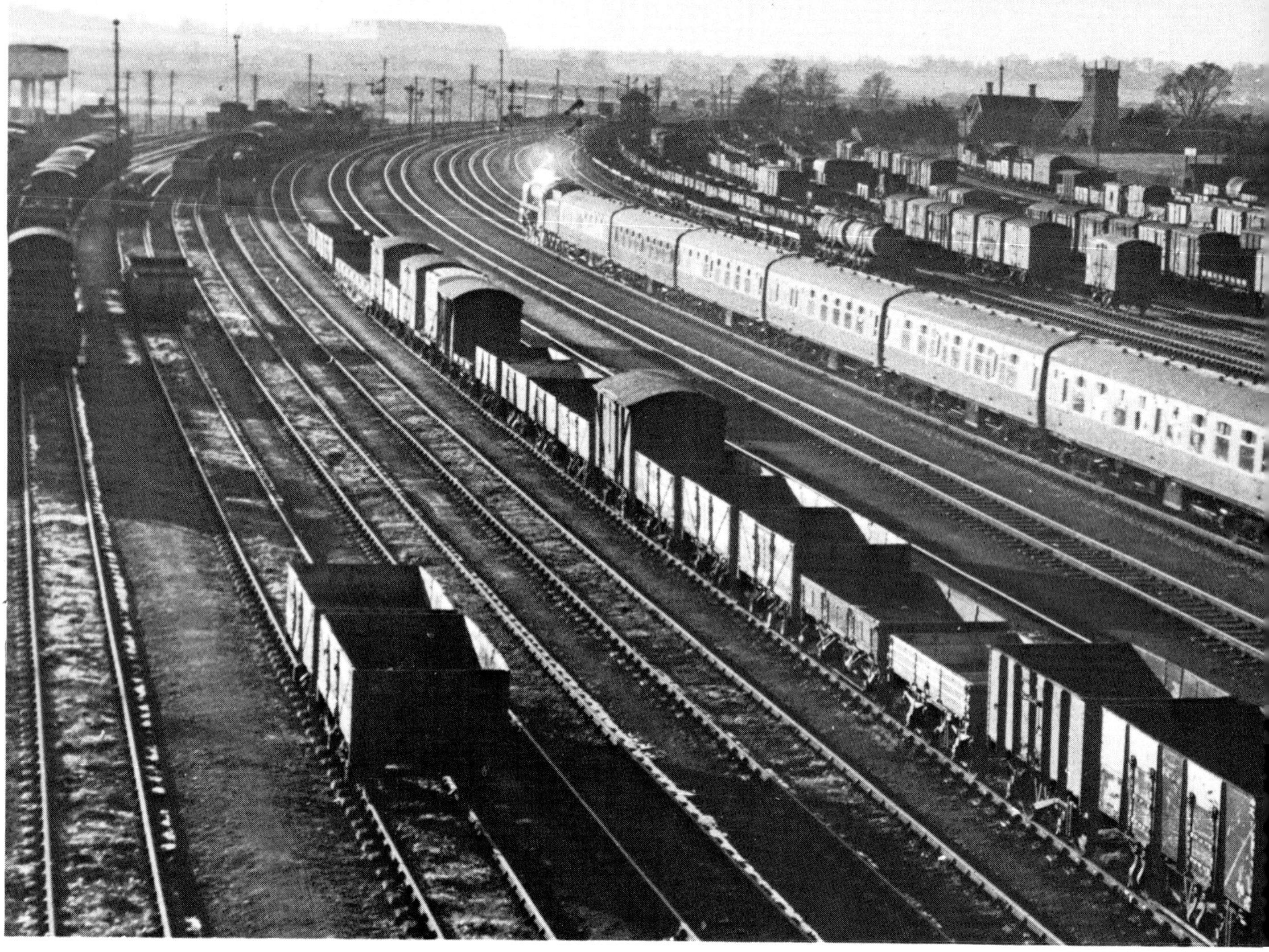

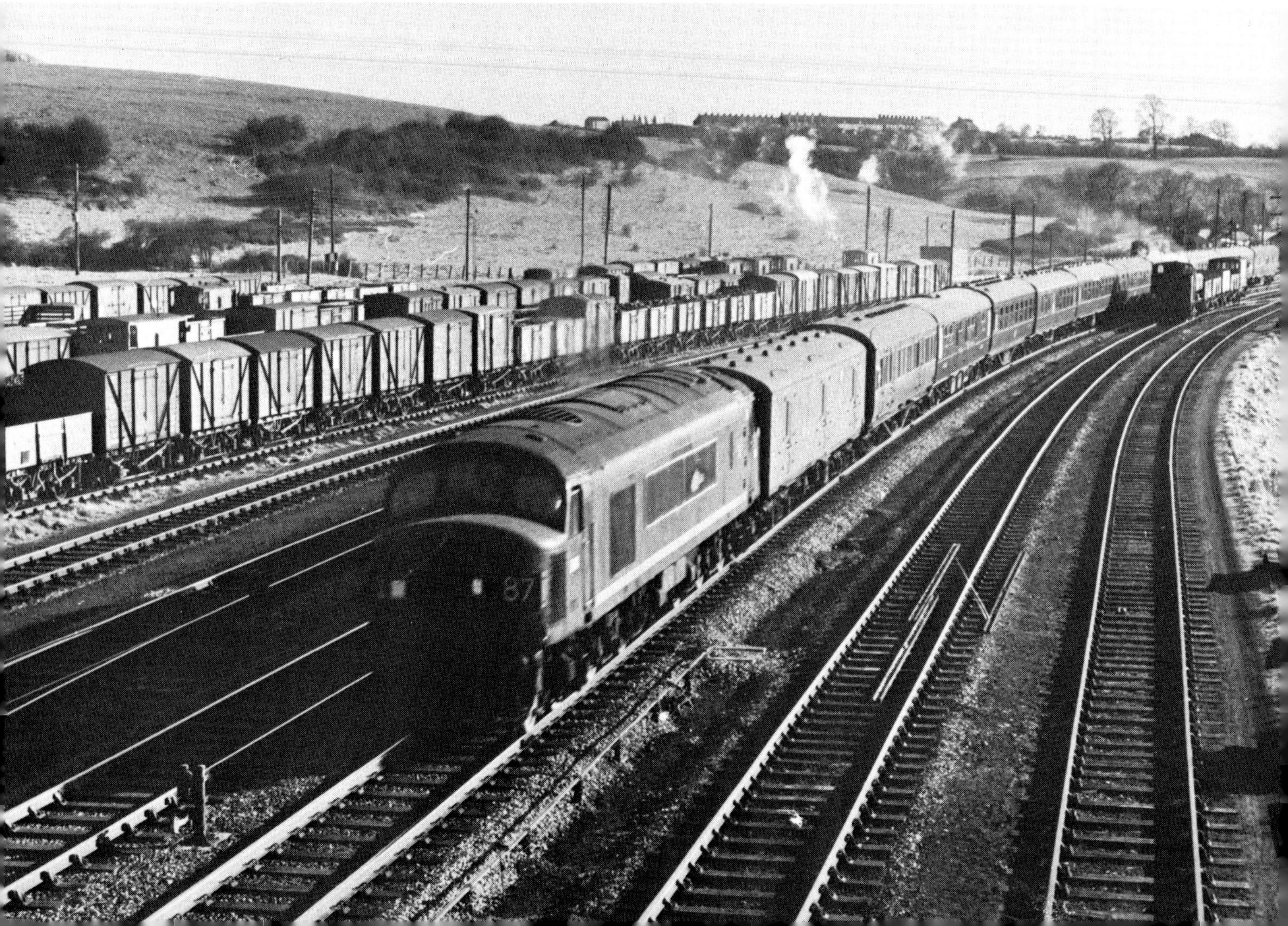

Left: Stoke Gifford marshalling yards re-echo to the clickety-clack of the 1.55pm Paddington-Pembroke Dock express headed by a 'Britannia' Pacific, as she eases off for the curve into Patchway Junction, on extreme right of picture in February 1958.

Below left: The 4.45pm Bristol-York passes Westerleigh yards in the early 1960s headed by a Class 45 diesel.

Below: A rare visitor to Bristol is rebuilt 'Scot' No 46161 *Kings Own*, racing down through Westerleigh yards at 80mph with a Newcastle-Bristol express in the last days of steam.

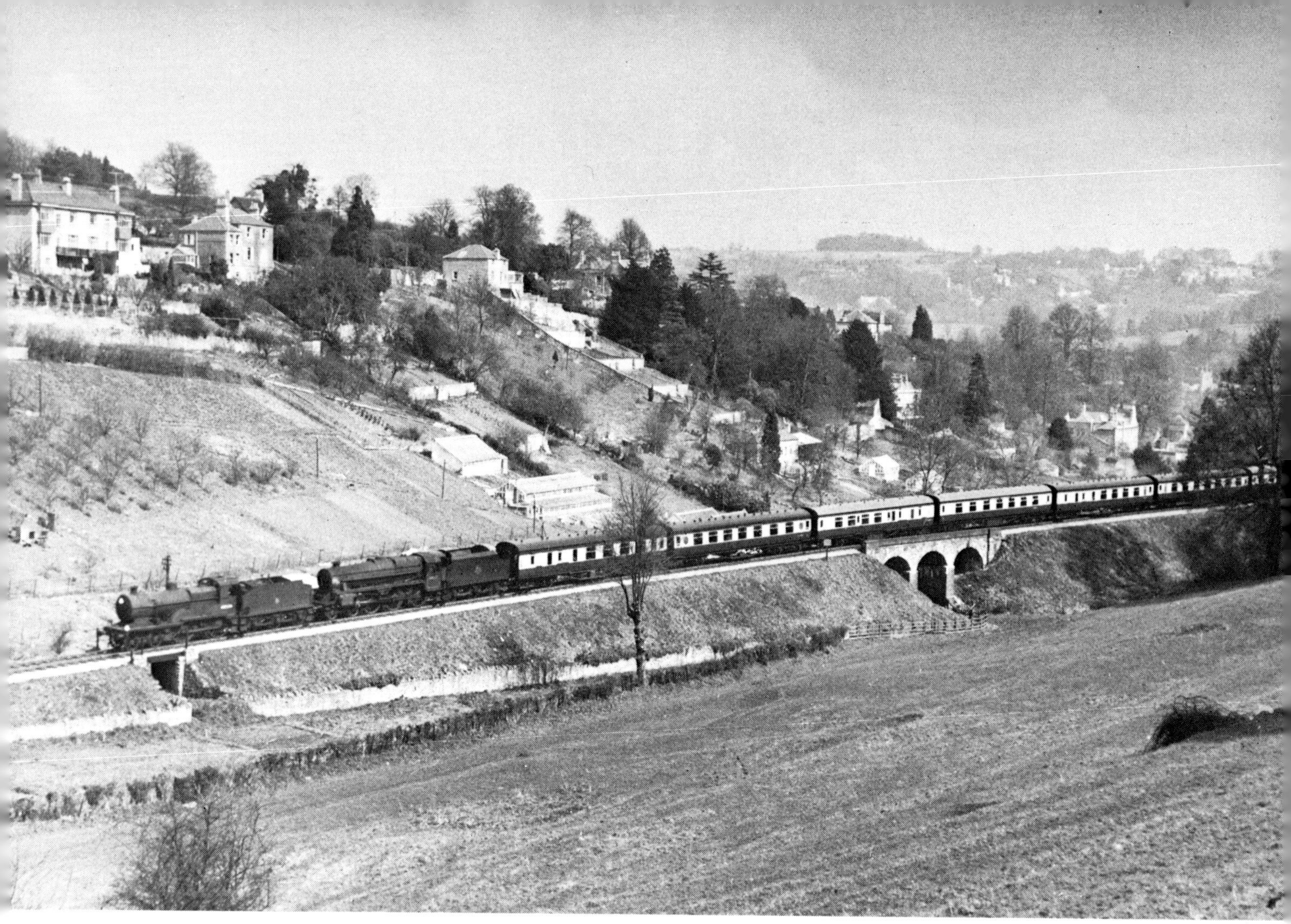

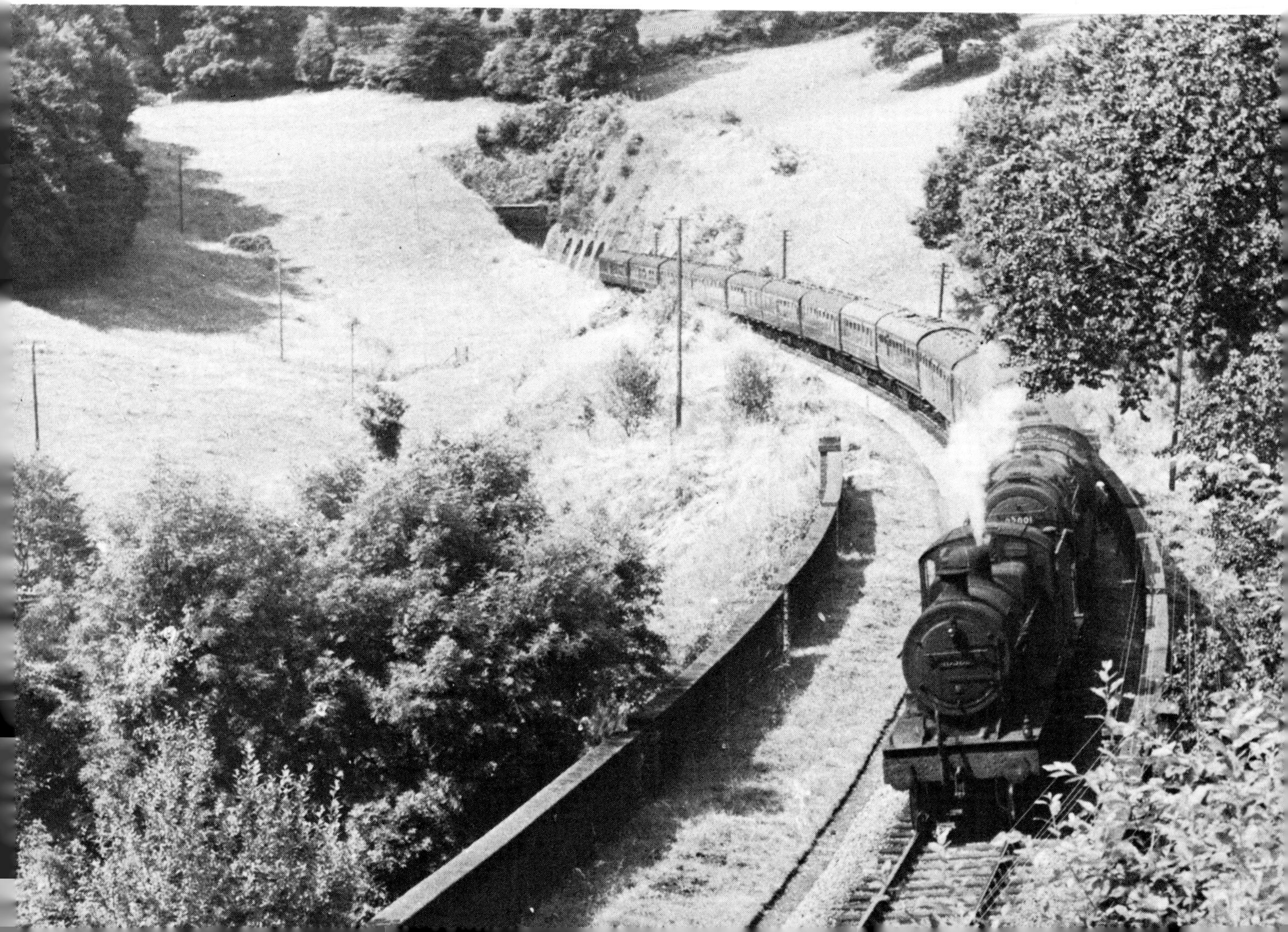

Left: The northbound 'Pines Express', doubleheaded over the Somerset & Dorset line by a Class 2P 4-4-0 and a Class 5 4-6-0, rolls downgrade from Combe Down Tunnel to Bath in April 1954.

Below left: Another view of the southbound 'Pines Express' leaving Combe Down Tunnel and taking Monkton Combe Viaduct behind a BR Class 9 2-10-0, piloted by an ex-Midland 2P 4-4-0.

Right: Devonshire Tunnel, south portal, outside Bath, with BR Standard Class 4 2-6-0 No 76014 emerging on an afternoon Bath Green Park-Templecombe stopping train on the S&D line.

Below: Stanier Class 5 4-6-0 No 44747 with Caprotti valve gear pulls out of Mangotsfield station with the 7.35am Bristol-Bradford express.

Above: A West-to-North cross-country express sets out from Bristol Temple Meads behind a 'Hall' class 4-6-0. In the background, going in the same direction, is a Bristol-Bath Green Park local train hauled by an Ivatt Class 2 2-6-2 tank.

Above right: 'County' class 4-6-0 No 1001 *County of Bucks* eases a Portsmouth-Cardiff express through Dr Day's Bridge Junction, Barton Hill, Bristol. In a few minutes she will make the scheduled halt at Stapleton Road station.

Right: A Shrewsbury-Plymouth express clatters over Dr Day's Bridge Junction at the eastern approaches to Bristol Temple Meads behind a 'County' class 4-6-0. Note the handsome 12-wheeled restaurant car.

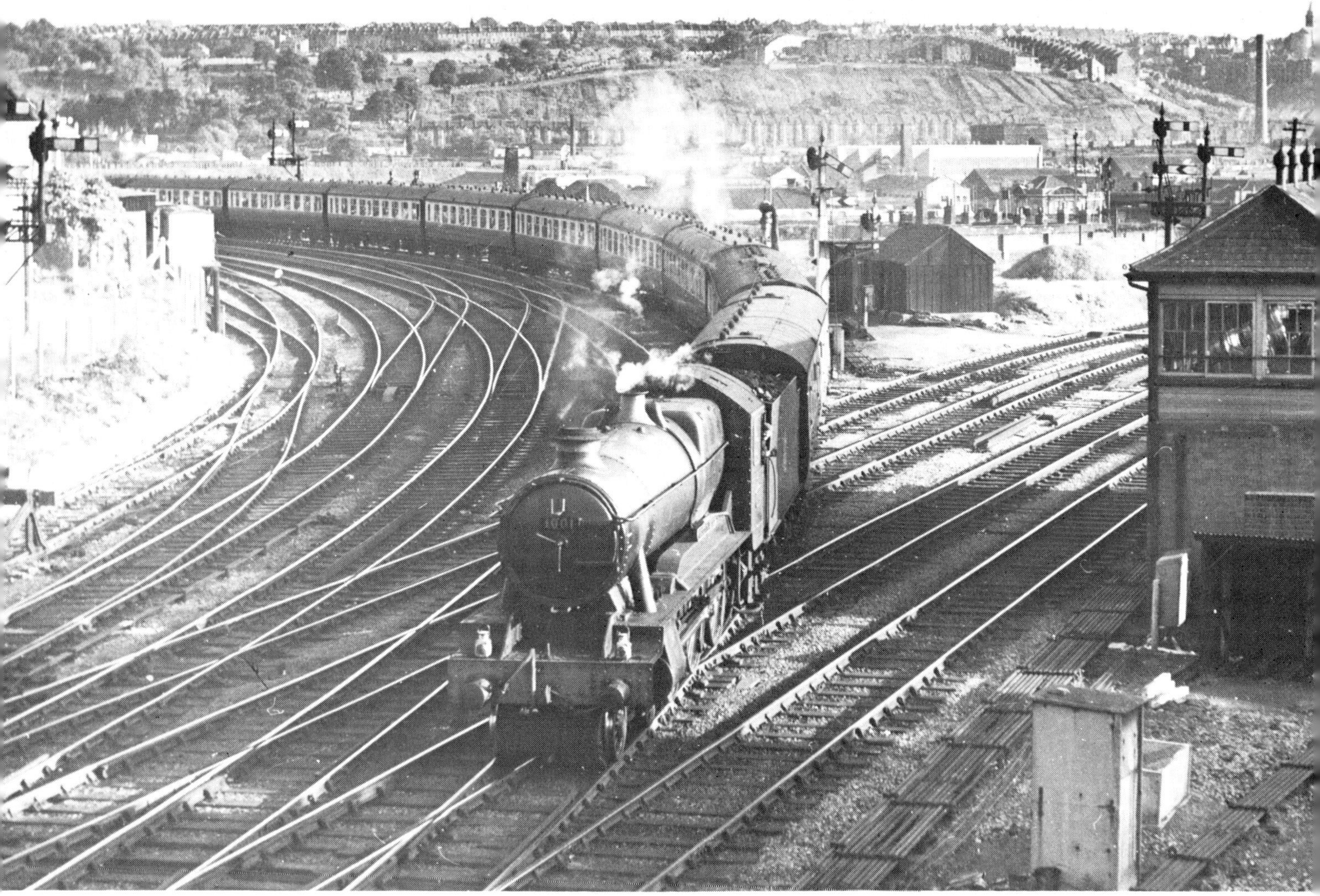

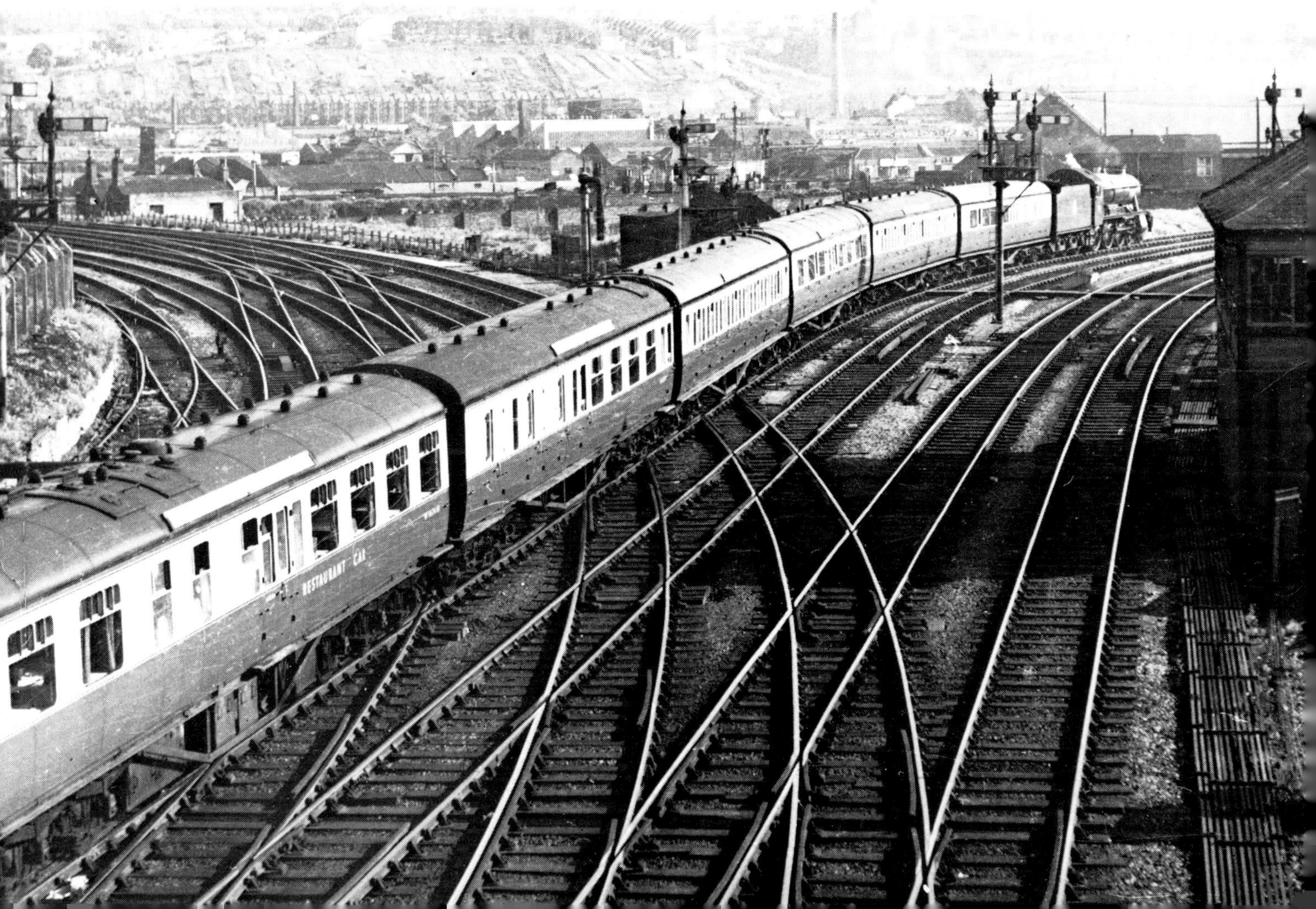
RESTAURANT

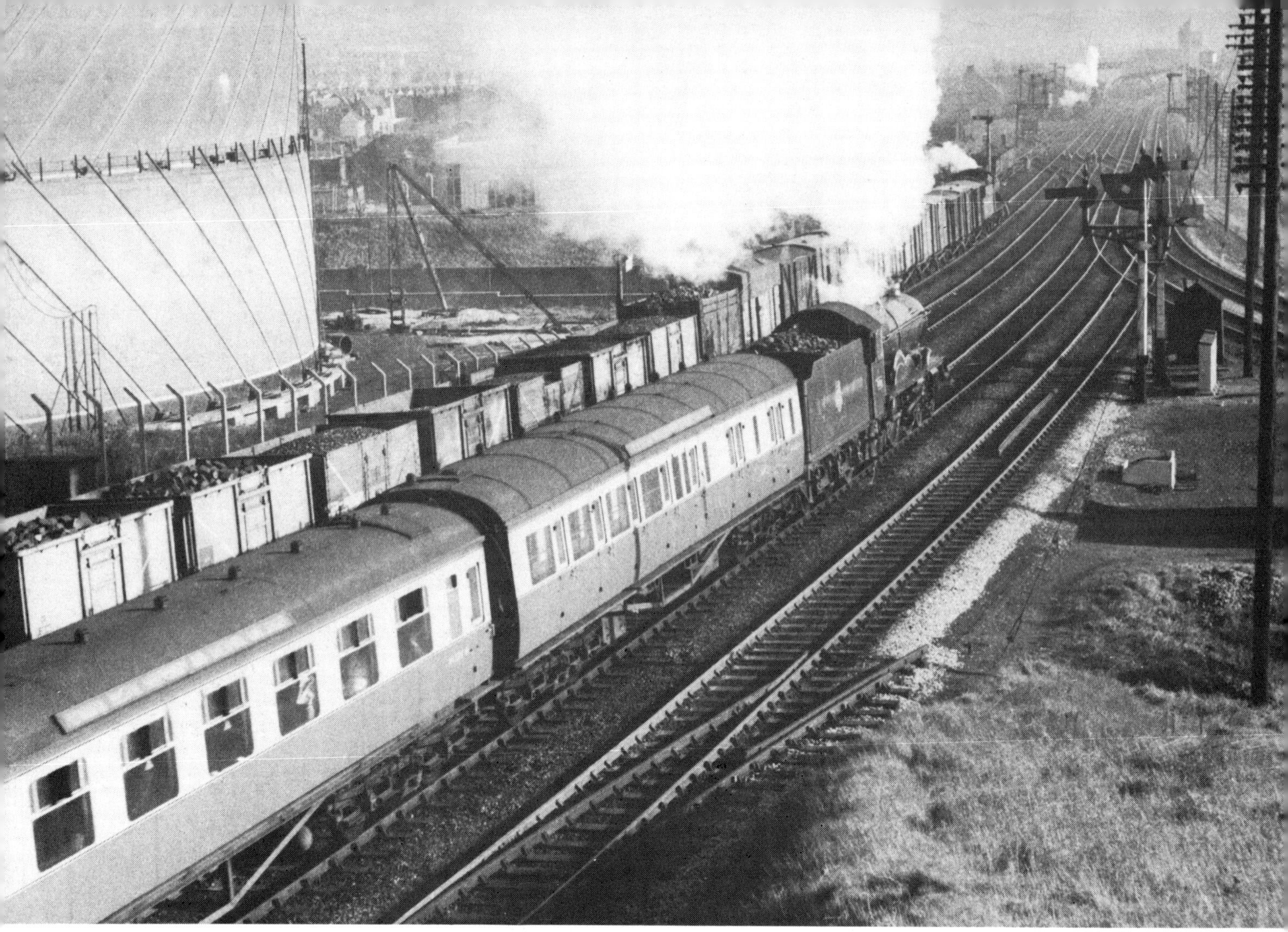

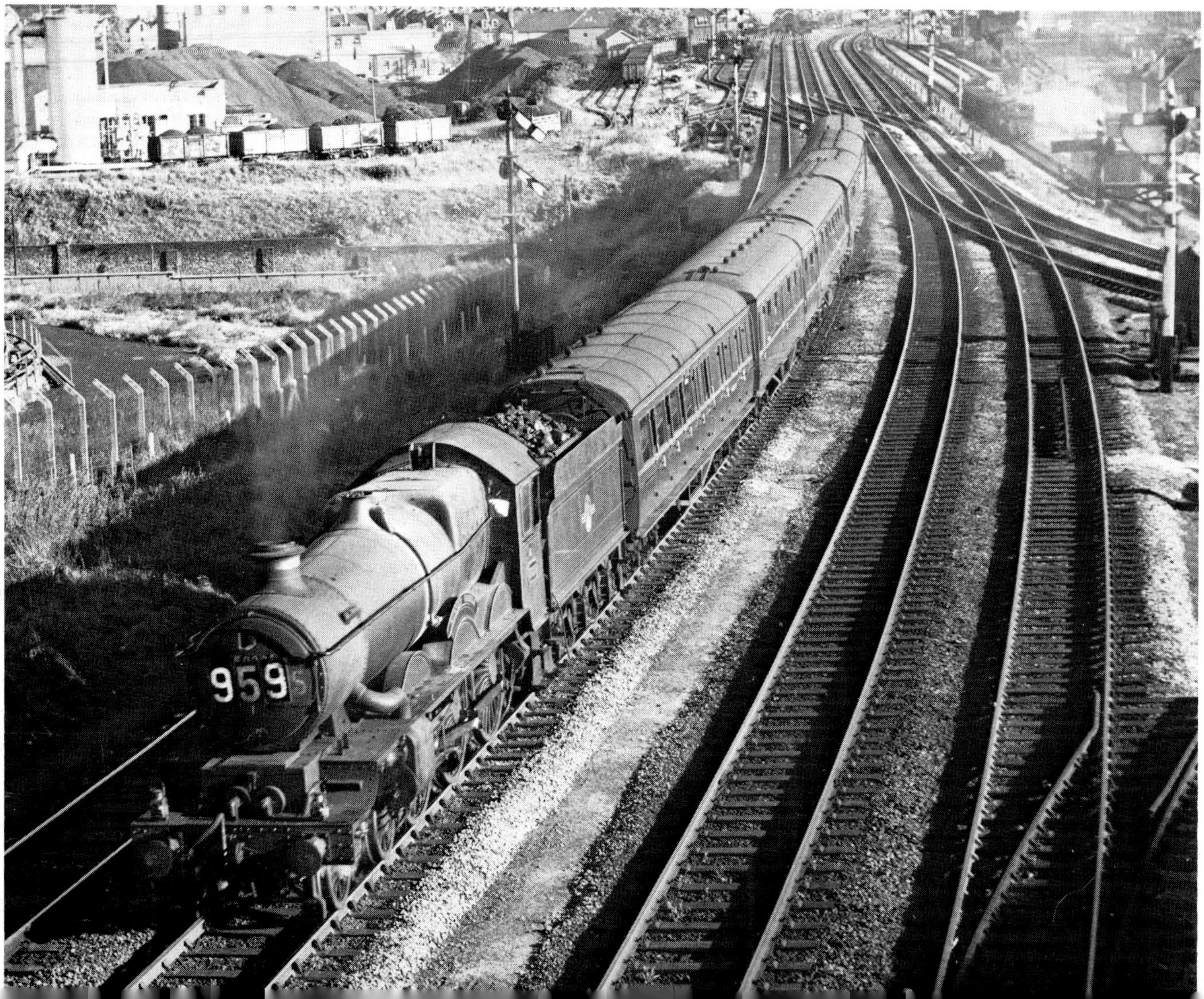
959

Above left: A Liverpool Lime Street-Shrewsbury-Bristol-Torquay express coasts down through Stapleton Road Junction on the outskirts of Bristol behind a 'Castle' 4-6-0 in 1955.

Left: No 5029 *Nunney Castle* passes Stapleton Road Junction and begins the climb to Filton with a Bristol-Liverpool train in August 1959.

Above: A busy scene at Bristol Stapleton Road Junction as two freights pass by, one behind 2-8-0T No 5236 beginning the 1 in 75 ascent to Filton Junction, assisted in the rear by the customary banker.

Left: A six-car dmu on the Bristol-Avonmouth service paces traffic on the Portway: photographed from the sea walls, Clifton Down, Bristol in May 1959.

Right: A Bristol-Birmingham Snow Hill express climbs through Narrowways Hill cutting, Ashley Hill, up to Filton Junction, headed by No 5035 *Coity Castle*.

Below: The eastbound 'Bristolian' forks right at Filton Junction to join the Badminton route to London at Stoke Gifford with a 'Castle' class 4-6-0 in charge.

Right: 'Jubilee' class 4-6-0 No 45602 *British Honduras* at platform 9, Bristol Temple Meads, with a West-to-North express in July 1964.

Below: Time for a cuppa while waiting for the right away at Temple Meads on 'Castle' No 5077 *Fairey Battle.*

Below right: A Saturday extra express for Birmingham pulls away from platform 7 Temple Meads behind BR Standard Class 5 4-6-0 No 73038.

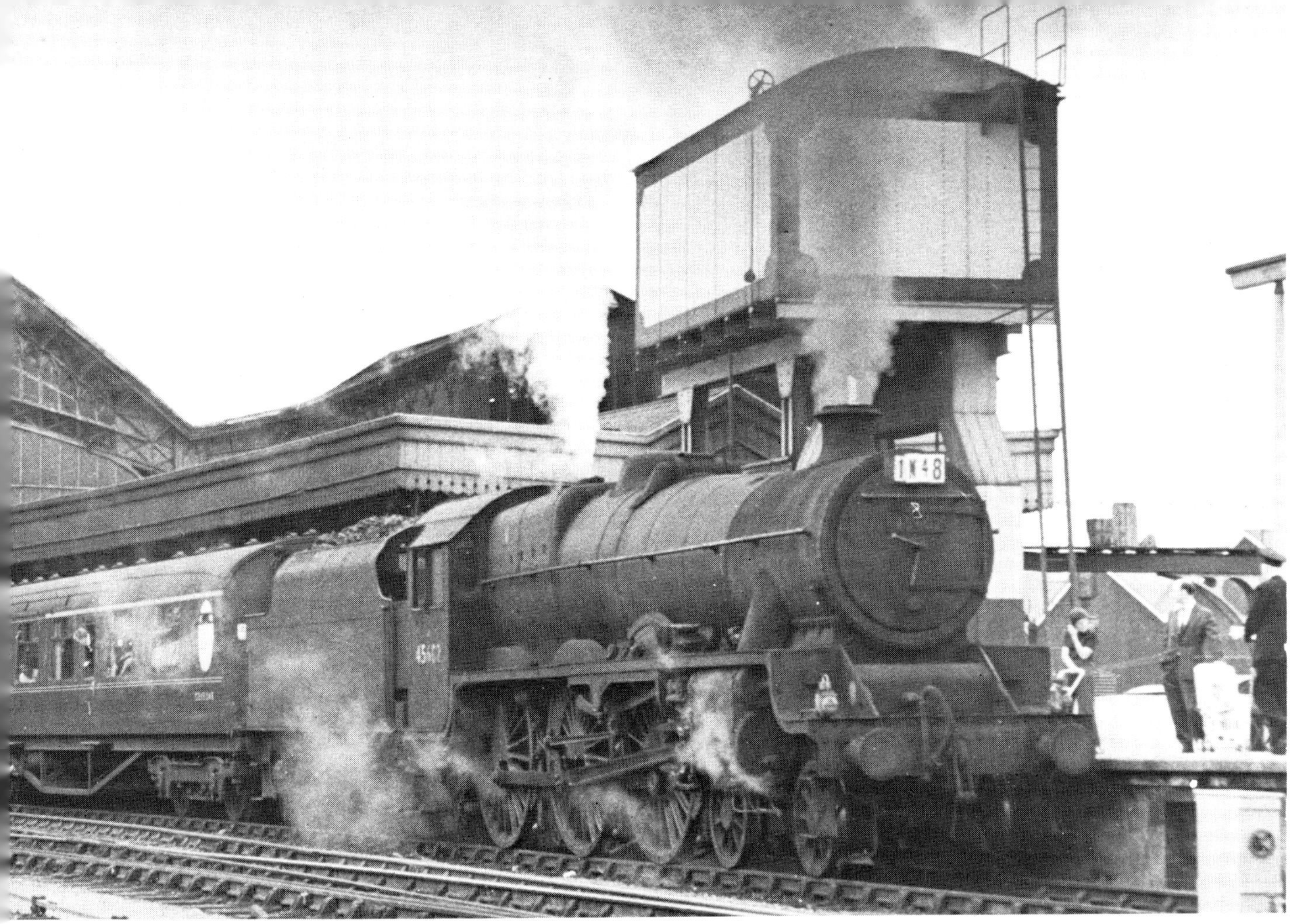
1N48

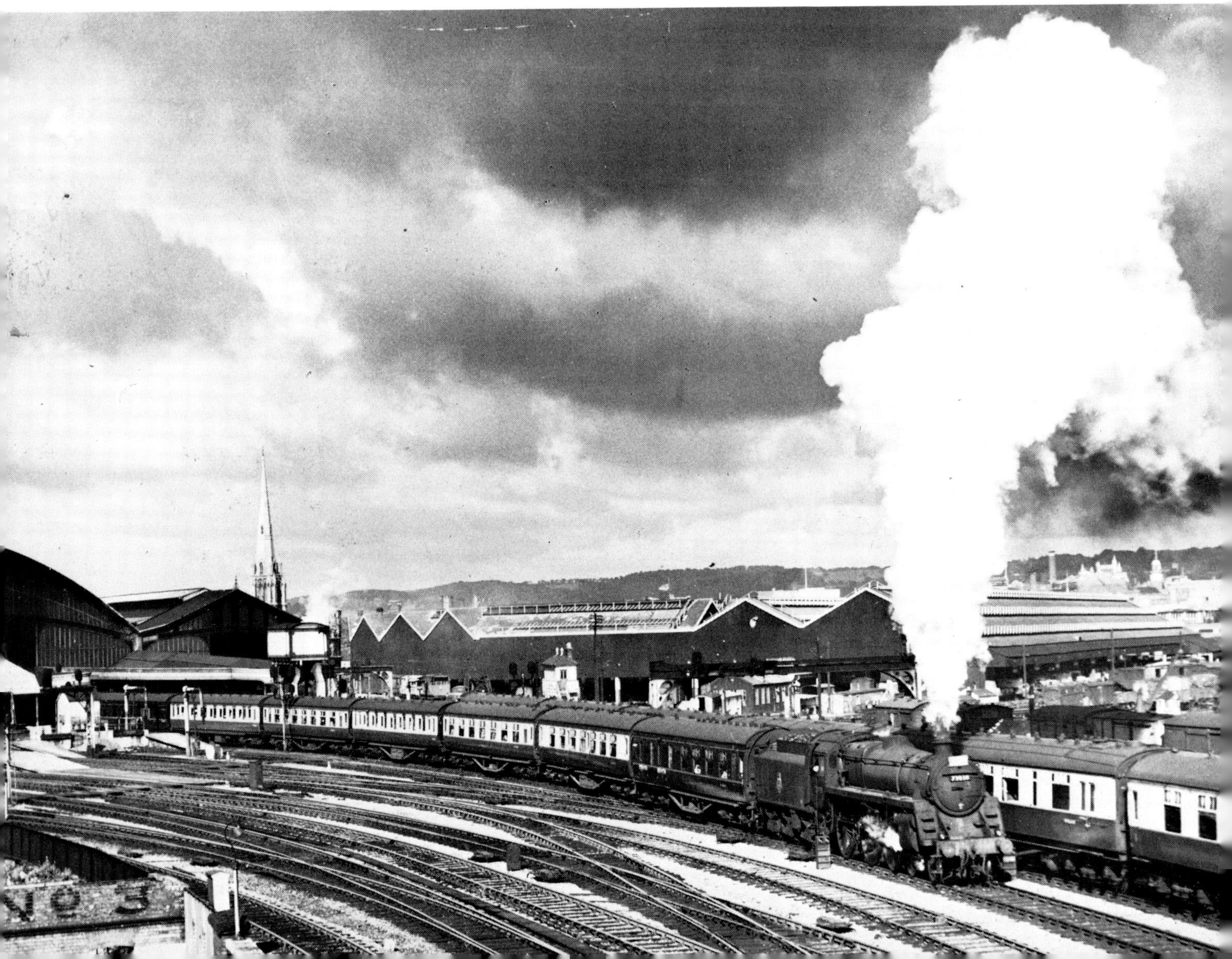
NO 3

Left: Evening sunlight illuminates the great booking hall of Bristol Temple Meads.

Below: No 7034 *Ince Castle* starts the 6.20pm express to Paddington out of platform 5, Bristol Temple Meads.

Right: Gleaming and handsome in the station lights, 'King' class 4-6-0 No 6007 *King William III* simmers at platform 5 Temple Meads with the 4.15pm Paddington-Plymouth express in January 1958.

'Western' class diesel No D1051 *Western Ambassador* glints under the lights of Bristol Temple Meads in December 1964.

Above: The southbound 'Cornishman' leaving Bristol Temple Meads behind 'Warship' diesel No D825 *Intrepid* in September 1962.

Below: Bristol Temple Meads in December 1976.

Above: Train No 107, the 12 noon to Paddington, pulls out of Bristol Temple Meads behind 'Castle' class 4-6-0 No 5082 *Swordfish* on a summer day in 1953.

Below: Immaculate in a shining new coat of blue, 'Western' class diesel No D1026 *Western Centurion* moves the 9.5am to Paignton out of Bristol Temple Meads in August 1967.

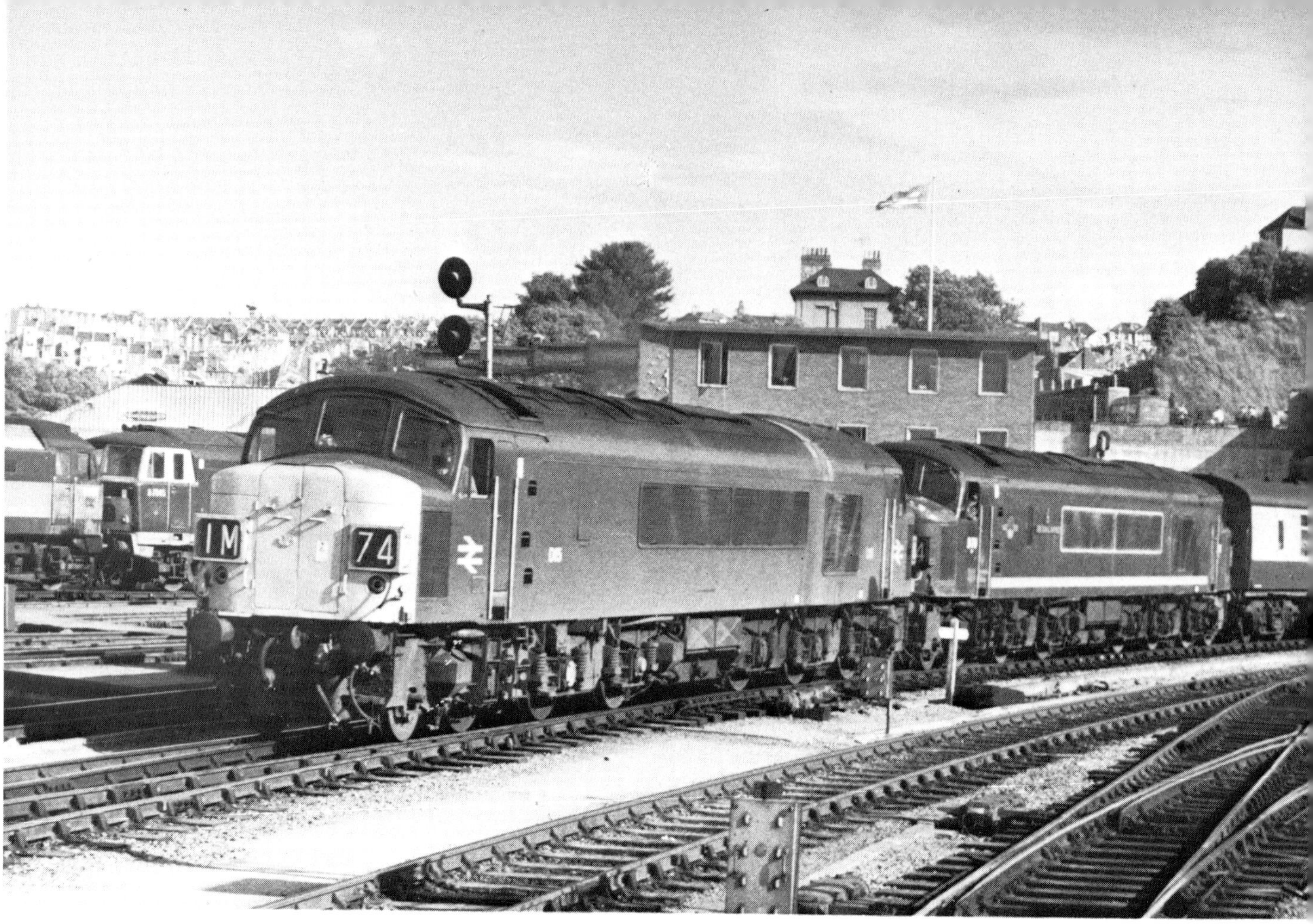
1M
74

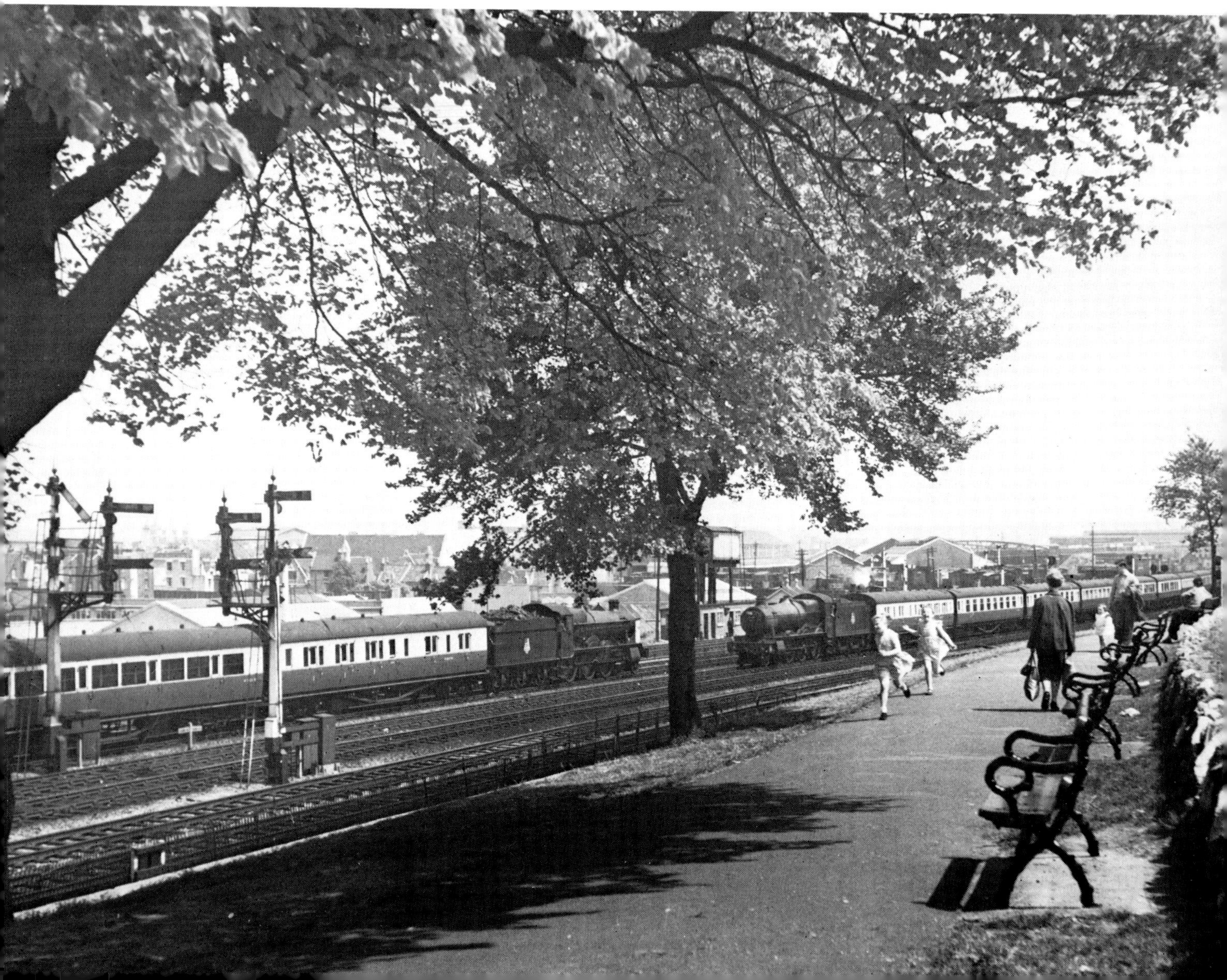

Left: With the squealing of flanges and chant of Sulzer diesel motors Class 45 diesel Nos D15 and D70 *The Royal Marines* ease a Paignton-Birmingham express under Bath Road Bridge and into platform 6, Bristol Temple Meads.

Below left: 'Hall' 4-6-0s pass at Bedminster Park, Bristol, looking towards Temple Meads.

Below: A Class 47 diesel-electric on a West-to-North express eases up the final approaches to Bristol Temple Meads on a summer Saturday in August 1967.

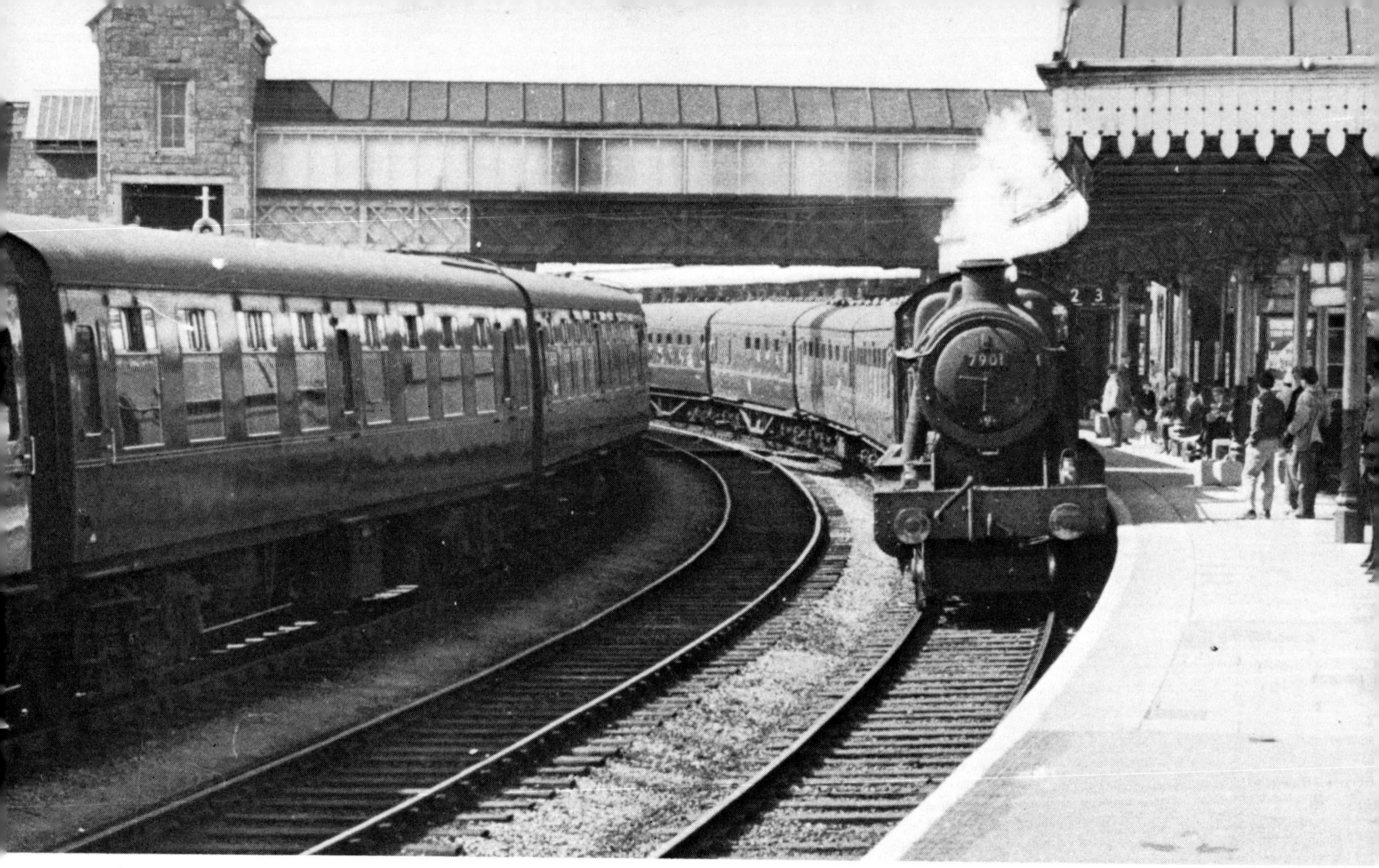
7901

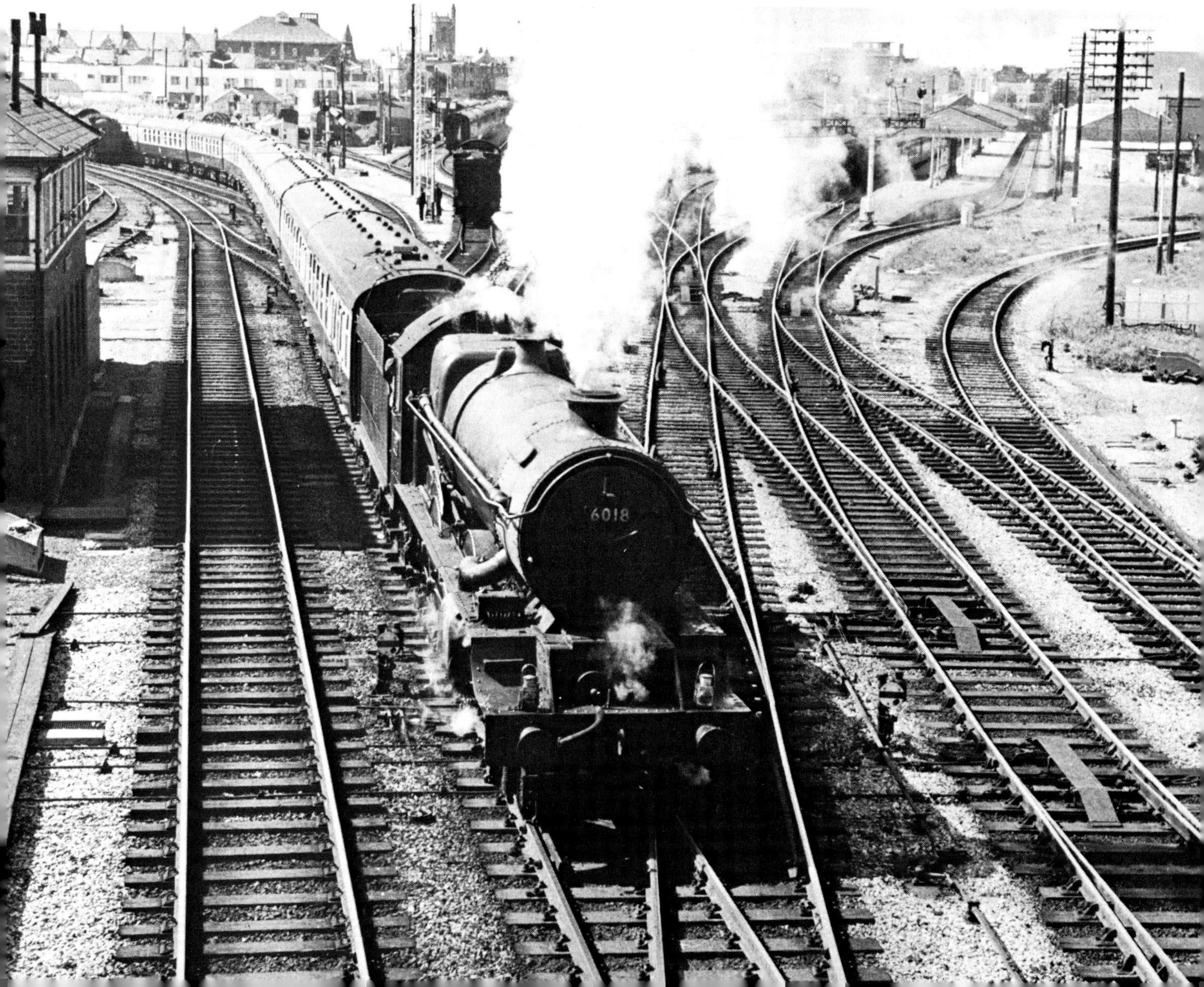
6018

Left: WR 4-6-0 No 7901 *Dodington Hall* pulls into Weston-super-Mare General with a Paignton-Wolverhampton holiday train comprising LM stock.

Below left: On summer days when Weston-super-Mare was as busy as London's main line stations, thousands passed through the gates of both the General and Locking Road stations. Here 'King' class 4-6-0 No 6018 *King Henry VI* moves a chocolate and cream-liveried express out of Weston-super-Mare General for Bristol and London.

Right: Busy scene at Weston-super-Mare in June 1961.

Below: 'Jubilee' 4-6-0 No 45564 *New South Wales* pulls out of Locking Road, Weston-super-Mare, with the 12.15pm to Sheffield in July 1963.

Above left: 'Castle' 4-6-0 No 5061 *Earl of Birkenhead* presents a stirring spectacle, standing with safety valves roaring in Cardiff General station in the late 1950s on a Swansea-Bristol express.

Left: The eastbound 'South Wales Pullman' emerges from Patchway Tunnel behind 4-6-0 No 7028 *Cadbury Castle* in May 1958.

Above: The vibrating ground ripples the water in the troughs as 'Britannia' Pacific No 70024 *Vulcan* rushes down from Sodbury Tunnel with the westbound 'Capitals United Express' in May 1961.

REPAIRERS
A.A. & R.A.C.
NEWPORT MON. MOTOR Coy LTD
SERVICE
DEPOT

5224

Left: The eastbound 'Red Dragon' crosses the River Usk behind a 'Britannia' Pacific on the way out of Newport in June 1958.

Below left: WR 2-8-0T No 5224 enters Newport station with a mineral train.

Below: A Bristol-bound express headed by a 'Hall' 4-6-0 pulls out of Newport behind the ruined castle on the banks of the Usk.

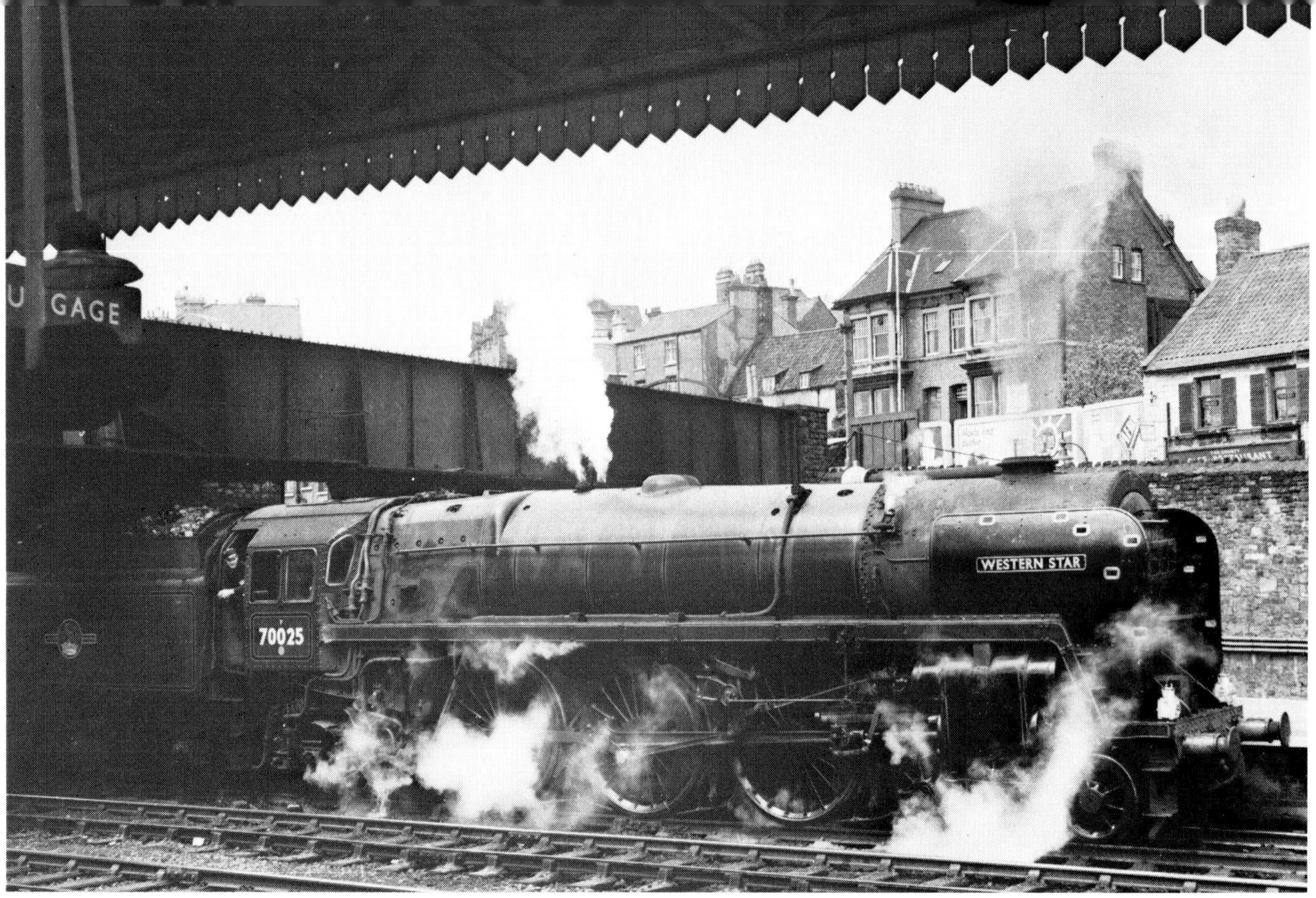
WESTERN STAR
70025

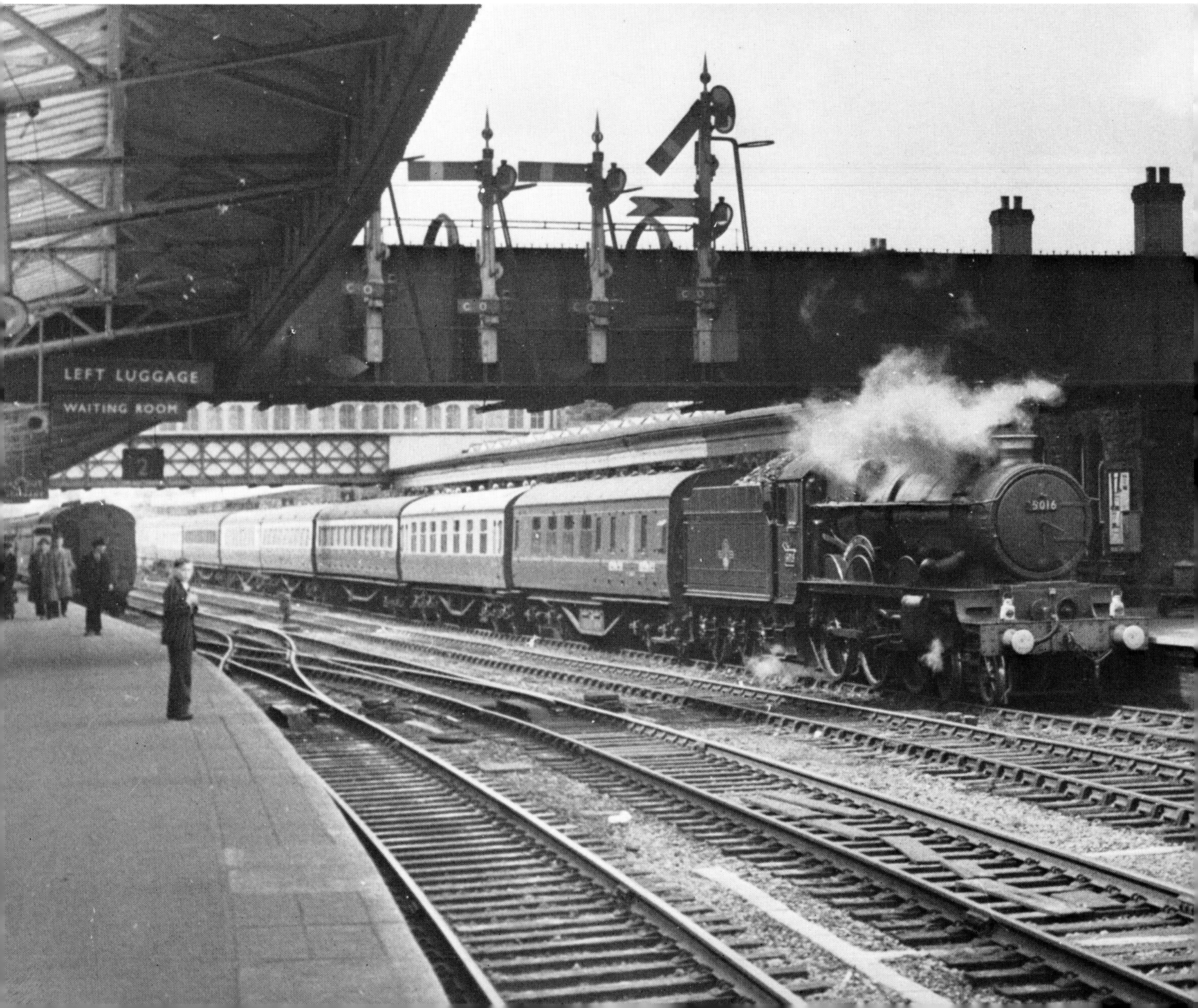
LEFT LUGGAGE
WAITING ROOM
5016

Above left: 'Britannia' Pacific No 70025 *Western Star* at Newport on a Pembroke Dock-Paddington express.

Left: Ancient and modern modes of transport at Newport station with 'Castle' class 4-6-0 No 5016 *Montgomery Castle* on the 12.50pm Cardiff-Portsmouth and a diesel set for Blaenavon awaiting departure.

Above: The 6.5pm Bristol-Cardiff leaving Newport behind 4-6-0 No 6919 *Tylney Hall*.

Above: A heavy coal train rumbles into Newport West behind 0-6-2 tank No 6600, followed on the far side of the cutting by a diesel train from Brynmawr.

Above right: The 8.55am Paddington-Neyland express goes underground west of Newport, past 0-6-0PT No 8499. In the background a WR 0-6-2T emerges from the tunnel.

Right: The 11.10am Milford Haven-Paddington approaching Newport in rainy weather behind a 'Castle' 4-6-0.

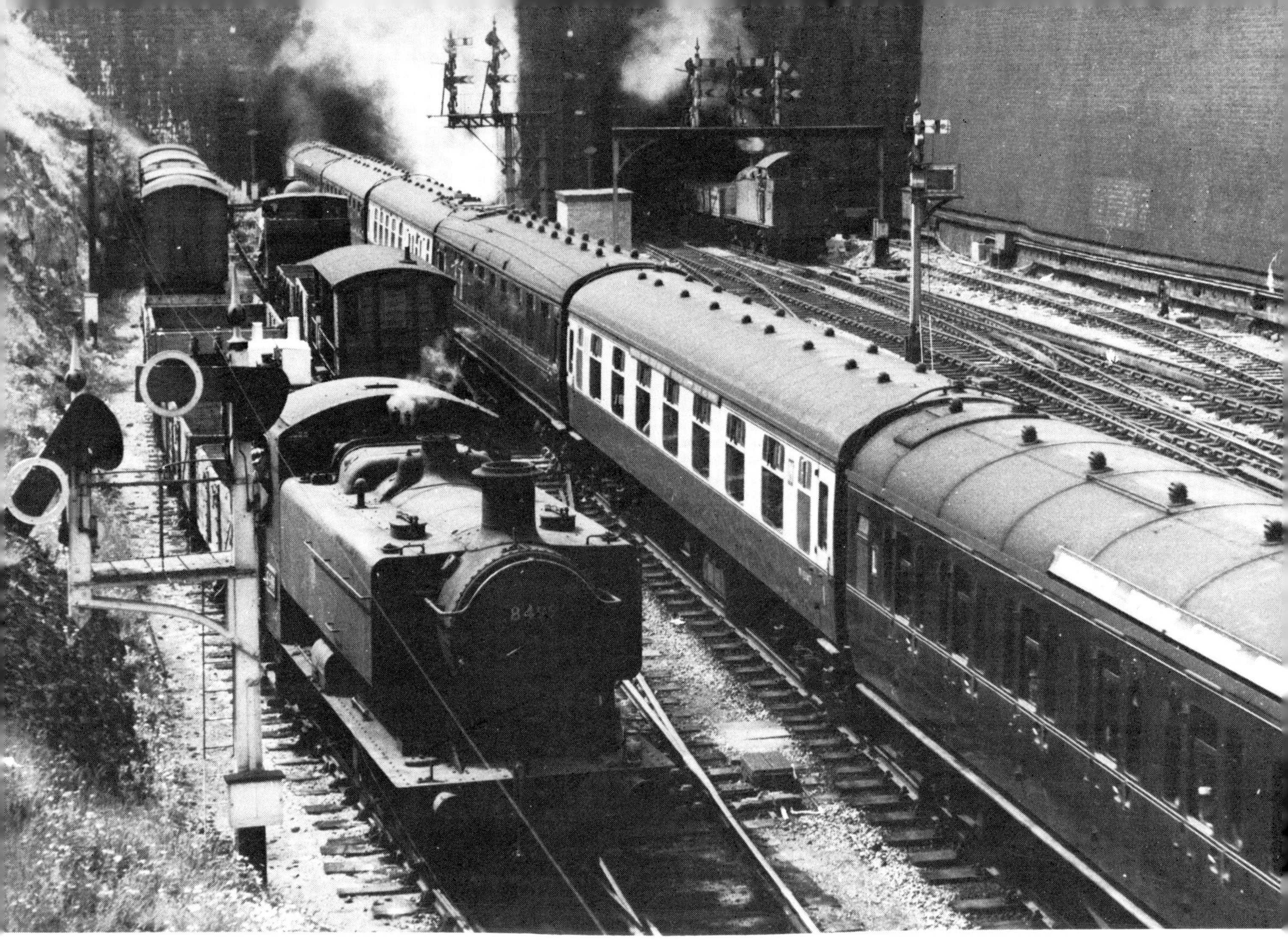

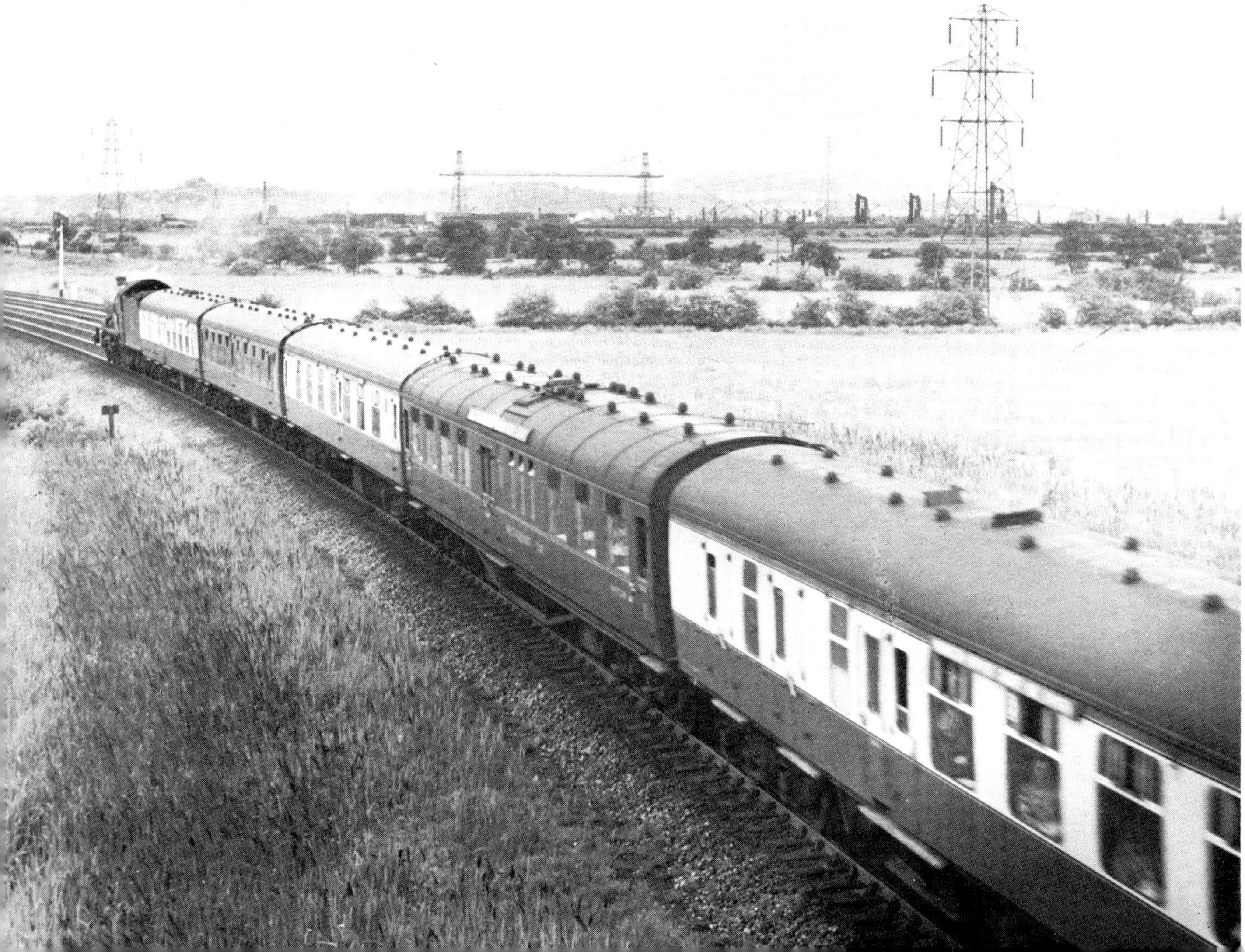

Right: WR 4-6-0 No 1029 *County of Worcester* approaches Cardiff General from the west with a parcels train.

Below: Stanier Class 5 No 45340 passes under the viaduct carrying the Paddington-South Wales main line at Westerleigh with a Gloucester-Bristol train.

Below right: WR 4-6-0 No 7028 *Cadbury Castle* accelerates past Pengam yards with the up 'South Wales Pullman' in July 1958.

Right: A Devon-bound Saturday special clatters briskly past Pengam yards behind No 6927 *Ulford Hall.*

Below: The 7.50am Fishguard Harbour to Paddington express gathers speed through Pengam yards behind 'Britannia' Pacific No 70029 *Shooting Star* in August 1958.

Below right: 'Castle' class 4-6-0 No 7001 *Sir James Milne* passing Pengam yards on the way into Cardiff with a Paddington-Swansea express.

Above: 'Castle' class 4-6-0 No 5077 *Fairey Battle* quenches her thirst at Cardiff General before continuing the journey to London with the 2.20pm from Milford Haven.

Below: WR 2-6-0 No 6323 rumbles towards Cardiff past Newtown West goods box with a freight train.

Above right: 'Britannia' Pacific No 70016 *Ariel* rumbles east past Newtown East box with the 7.50am Fishguard-Paddington.

Right: Pengam power station and railway yards with a passing BR Standard Class 4 4-6-0.

Above: Smoky scene at Canton shed with Nos 1022 *County of Northampton* and 5970 *Hengrave Hall* coaled and oiled up ready for action.

Below: Locomotives ready for duty at Cardiff Canton sheds; in the foreground are WD 2-8-0 No 90201 and Class 9 2-10-0 No 92222.

Above: A WD 2-8-0 leads a BR Standard Class 5 4-6-0 and Class 7 Pacific No 70026 *Polar Star* out of Canton to duty.

Below: A study in boilers at Cardiff Canton sheds.

Above: Two generations of diesels are represented here as a new HST pulls up alongside Class 52 diesel-hydraulic No 1023 *Western Fusilier* at Paddington in October 1976.

Below: A 'Western' class diesel-hydraulic traverses the scenic coastal route between Dawlish and Teignmouth with a Paddington-Penzance express in August 1974.